CW00422098

MY SPORTING LIFE

MY SPORTING LIFE
Willis Hall

Illustrations by Bill Tidy

William Luscombe

First published in Great Britain by
William Luscombe Publisher Ltd.
The Mitchell Beazley Group
Artists House
14 Manette Street
London WIV 5LB
1975

© 1975 by WILLIS HALL

All rights reserved. No part of
this publication may be reproduced, stored in
a retrieval system, or transmitted, in
any form or by any means, electronic,
mechanical, photocopying, recording
or otherwise, without the prior permission
of the Copyright owner.

ISBN 0 86002 091 6

Printed in Great Britain by
Cox & Wyman Ltd.,
London, Fakenham and Reading

CONTENTS

ACKNOWLEDGEMENTS

Acknowledgements and thanks are due to the following publications and Television companies:

To *Sportsworld* for *Sports Days, No Legs Eleven, Child's Play, How My Style Was Cramped, There's No Business . . . , Another Christmas Carol, Representative Honours, Hanging Them Up, Dear Mr Revie, World Cup 74, Away From It All* and *England's Boss.*

To the *Evening Standard* for *Stormy Weather, Whistle And I'll Come To You, A Matter of Priorities, Bigmal And Billy-Goat Cluff, Giant-Killing, A Load Of Old Analysis, Humble Fare* and *For Best Or For Worse.*

To *Elephanta* for *The Good Boardroom Guide.*

To BBC Television for the extracts from *They Don't All Open Men's Boutiques, Song At Twilight* and *Illegal Approach.*

To Granada Television for the extract from *Friendly Encounter.*

To ATV for the extract from *The Piano-Smashers of the Golden Sun.*

To Victor Gollancz for the extract from *The Evacuees.*

1 INTRODUCTION

In some ways, it hasn't been a bad old sporting life, taking the ups with the downs – even though there have probably been more downs than ups. There was the time, for instance, when Sir Alf Ramsey, at that point in charge of the England team, ignored me completely – it happened when I sat opposite him in a train compartment going up to Stoke one Wednesday and we never exchanged a word throughout the journey. But there you go, that's all part and parcel of being one of soccer's nonentities.

So why write a book about it, you ask? When the sporting field of the literary world is already crammed with the disclosures of international players and the shocking biographies of world-famous managers, who am I to rush into print with my feeble anecdotes?

Well, it hasn't been entirely humdrum – I've had my moments. There was the occasion, for instance, when I picked up a trophy at Wembley. No, not quite an F A Cup-winner's medal, but at least a silver-plated candlestick, by proxy, for a greyhound of mine that won a 525 yard race in the famous stadium. And then there was the time when I carried Sir Stanley Matthews' boots for him. And how many people can lay claim to having massaged Billy Wright's duff knee during a half-time interval? Also, for those who may be interested, I am able to reveal exactly what it was that Big Jack Charlton said to me about football and the theatrical profession. Or how about the occasion when I was carried off the field with cramp during the second half of a friendly match inside an open prison? If the prospect of these and a myriad other explosive revelations intrigue you, read on. . . .

2 SPORTS DAYS

'You know that I want a pair of plimsolls for this after-noon, don't you?' shouted my six-year-old over the blare of Radio One and the staccato snap-crackle-and-popping of his breakfast.

The announcement threw me for several seconds – whenever the lad asks for anything that has the mildest sporting connotation, it is tantamount to hearing the Chief Rabbi order a pork sandwich.

'In God's name, *what for?*' I managed at last.

'For the school Sports Day.'

'What school Sports Day?'

'*My* school Sports Day. This afters. I *told* you. *Ages* ago. You *promised* you'd come.' His voice had risen an octave, partly because he was close to tears and partly to make himself heard above his younger brother who was making racing-car noises.

'Don't make racing-car noises at the table,' I said to the three-year-old, 'you've been told about that a dozen times.' I turned back to the elder boy. He was right. He had told me about his forthcoming school Sports Day and, naturally, I had forgotten. Mentally, I rearranged a vitally necessary script conference for a T V series and also excused myself from an important lunch at an exclu-sive restaurant club with an American film producer – in order to attend a series of foot races at a place of educa-tion for Junior Mixed Infants. A promise is a promise. I said aloud:

'And don't sniffle either. If I said I'd come – I'll come. And what happened to your old plimsolls?'

'Somebody pinched them. I *told* you. *Ages* ago.'

'I don't know why you can't put your name in your plimsolls like everybody else.'

'What with?' he said with interest.

'An indelible pencil. What size plimsolls?'

'Eleven-and-a-halfs. What's an indelible pencil?'

'Shut up and eat your breakfast.'

Silence – save for snapping-and-crackling-and-popping . . .

Which explains why I came to be sitting in the middle of a draughty field on a chair apparently fashioned for a midget, along with a heterogeneous collection of similarly seated Adult Mixed Parents, on a dull grey day in late July.

I had already had an altercation with a gentleman in a shoe shop:

'You can have eleven or twelves, sir?'

'I want eleven-and-a-halfs.'

'Plimsolls don't come in half-sizes, sir.'

'That's utterly ridiculous! I bet if they were for David Bedford you'd have half-sizes!'

'But they aren't, are they, sir? If they were, they wouldn't be plimsolls – they'd have spikes in.'

I was sitting in the middle of a field on a midget's chair clutching a pair of size twelve plimsolls in my right hand and keeping a tight rein on my three-year-old son with my left. I was left holding the plimsolls because I had been informed that I wasn't allowed to approach my six-year-old until *after* the races. I was restraining my three-year-old because he had insisted on coming with me. He had somehow got it fixed in his mind that 'races' meant that he was going to see Emerson Fittipaldi and the John Player Special

I was waving the size twelve plimsolls above my head in an effort to attract the attention of the six-year-old, who was with the rest of his class on the other side of the field. I was nursing a vain hope that if I wasn't allowed to approach him, perhaps it would be acceptable to the teaching staff if *he* approached *me*. As I waved the plimsolls insanely, I was almost jerked off my midget chair by the three-year-old, straining at the leash. With him it had become a case of the mountain going to Mahomet – he had had enough of waiting and wanted to drift off alone across the field in search of Emerson Fittipaldi and/either/or the John Player Special.

And I apologize if the above paragraph all sounds a bit frenetic. School Sports Days tend to be a bit like that. Frenetic.

And though modern education, I am the first to admit, has come on by leaps and bounds since I last stretched my legs under a school desk, school Sports Days don't seem to have altered one iota.

Something rather strange and horrible seems to come over school teachers on Sports Days. Schoolmasters sport old-fashioned flannel trousers and stride about purposely, lording it over Adult Mixed Parents. Schoolmistresses, who are attractive and desirable for 364 days of the year, on Sports Days don strange blazers with gold wire emblems, and go about bare-legged and goose-pimpled.

The actual events aren't any great shakes either – well, certainly not for Junior Mixed Infants.

Accepting the fact that my elder boy was only coming up for seven, I had not gone along that afternoon with any delusions. I had not, for instance, supposed that I was going to see him run the 1500-metre hurdles, or put the shot, or compete in a gruelling steeplechase. On the other hand, I did consider him suitable material for inclusion in, say, a juvenile 50-metre dash, or a kiddies' miniature long-jump.

I mean, after all, I ask you, why would I otherwise involve myself in a heated altercation with a shoe-shop assistant on the relative sizes of plimsolls?

However, I discovered that the lad was entered in a track event that I had not come across before, listed in my duplicated programme as:

3.45 p.m.; MRS BENSON'S NOVELTY RACE

Mrs Benson, it should be explained, is my six-year-old's current mentor.

The so-called novelty race that bore the good lady's name, it should be further explained, consisted of my lad and half a dozen of his unfortunate playmates being togged out in ladies' tights and running a distance of some thirty yards during which they had to pick up, *en route*, a number of cardboard egg cartons and stuff them down the tights in transit.

I strongly suspect that 'Mrs Benson's Novelty Race' owes more in its origination to *It's A Knockout* than it does to Olympic track competition.

It was not immediately apparent after the race whether the winner was the Juvenile Mixed Infant to breast the tape first or the one that had accumulated the most egg cartons. A simple mental calculation forced me to the opinion that, on aggregate, my boy had come last in a field of six.

Immediately after the race, he turned and looked across the field to where I sat. Was he seeking sympathy, I wondered, or was there recrimination in his glance? After all, he had had to run the race in his ordinary shoes while I had sat clutching the new plimsolls. But the smile he gave me was positively beatific. Losing at competitive sport was not a new experience for him. Not only that, but I am the father of a boy who has brought the art of being a good loser to the highest pinnacle of sporting endeavour. In some ways, you've got to admire him for it.

Not so the three-year-old.

The three-year-old does not accept defeat gracefully. The three-year-old sulks. At least, either the three-year-old sulks or he stamps his feet relentlessly with an innate sense of insane compulsion.

With this in mind, I had some grim foreboding of trouble when one of the masters (instantly recognizable by his clip-board and his flannel trousers) approached a captive group of us Adult Mixed Parents, huddled together for warmth and security on our midget chairs, and suggested adding an extra event to the afternoon's programme – an Invitation Race for visiting Nursery Mixed Toddlers.

My three-year-old went into paroxysms of delight. With curling lip and some distaste, he had watched the total failure of his elder brother and felt that the onus was now upon himself to bring honour back to the family name.

I accompanied my youngest to the start-line where he joined some dozen or so more Nursery Mixed Toddlers, all straining at the leash of parenthood. The man in the flannel trousers with the clip-board lined them up, fussily, paused for dramatic effect then:

'On your marks . . . get set . . .'

A dozen or so Nursery Mixed Toddlers got on their marks and got set obediently. One Nursery Toddler - mine, naturally – neither got on his mark nor got set. He had decided that he *was* Emerson Fittipaldi in the John Player Special. He was clutching tight on an imaginary steering wheel and making very loud racing-car noises.

The man with the clip-board and flannels was trying hard to pretend that my three-year-old didn't exist.

'Get set. . . . GO!'

A dozen or so Nursery Mixed Toddlers hared off like competent milers for the finishing tape that was all of twenty yards away. My particular Nursery Mixed Toddler stood as if rooted to the ground, revving the engine of his John Player Special, turning his imaginary steering wheel and making racing-car noises as loudly as he could – which is pretty loud by any standards. All to no avail. By the time he had released his hand-brake and thrown the John Player Special into gear, the Mixed Toddlers' Invitation Race was over. The Halls had lost again.

Emerson Fittipaldi stamped his feet with an innate sense of insane compulsion and bawled his heart out at the start-line.

Men with clip-boards and flannels and ladies with

gold-wire badges and goose-pimples converged on the famous racing driver from all four corners of the field. By hard running and the sheerest of good luck, I got to him first.

I carried the three-year-old home, still howling, while the six-year-old born loser trotted at my side and tried to explain to his younger brother that you can't win them all. The younger brother believes that you can.

The size twelve plimsolls are too big for the six-year-old. The three-year-old wears them all the time these days. He puts them on over his own shoes and slops around the garden all day long at the wheel of the John Player Special. He is in training already for next year's Invitation Race at his brother's Junior Mixed Infants School.

Good luck to him! And I wish him every success.

I can't go next year, unfortunately. I have a vitally necessary script conference for a TV series and I'm lunching with an American film producer on the very day – I don't intend to duck either appointment.

3 NO LEGS ELEVEN

I have sat in on many a rousing argument, at every level from television studio debate to heated words in a saloon-bar bog, about why nobody has succeeded in making a cracking good fictional film with a soccer theme. Indeed, apart from Sydney Howard in *Up For The Cup*, a comic epic shot way back in 1933, the subject seems to have been left well alone. (Keen moviegoers will not need telling that the film titled *Arsenal*, made in the USSR in 1929, concerns the workers' revolution and has nothing at all to do with the well-known football club that bears that name.)

And yet soccer, with its world-wide following, would seem ripe for transition to the big screen.

As I say, I have listened to pundits on both sides of the fence, to film makers and to soccer analysts, and the arguments they have put forward have been lucid, informed and innumerable. I have, in fact, stuck in my own intelligent two-penn'orth every now and then. But nobody has ever seemed to come up with a *satisfactory* answer to the question.

Nobody, at least, until I chatted on the subject to Jackie Charlton not long ago. And the solution is so obvious and simple that I've been kicking myself ever since.

'The fact is,' said Big Jack, 'that actors haven't got footballers' legs.'

He's dead right. They haven't. Not by any stretch of the imagination.

And even if they had, how in God's name would one set about casting them? Like they did it in those Alice

Faye-type pictures in the forties? You know the ones I mean, where the leering producer lines up a dozen or so glamorous cuties and invites them to hitch up their skirts. Modestly, for his and our benefits, the young ladies flash an exciting length of calf.

You could never invite actors to behave like that – it would look more like a weeding-out contest for a knobbly knees contest at a third-rate holiday camp.

Not, mark you, that I'm suggesting there is anything physically *wrong* with actors' legs. Perish the thought. On the contrary, generally speaking, they are mostly more than functional – put to the use for which they were intended.

Decked out in Elizabethan tights, hovering below a cod-piece, strutting across the boards at Stratford-upon-Avon, most actors' legs have seldom been known to fail to please – even when put to the test of being dodged about on in a duel scene at the National Theatre they have hardly ever been known to let their bearers down. But stick them in Umbro stockings and Adidas boots and ask them to show their paces on well-cut turf and all at once the faults begin to show through.

And I speak from bitter experience, for it's been my

unhappy lot to have to ask actors to portray footballers in more than one dramatic piece for television. Finding actors who *think* they can imitate footballers is not difficult. Most actors are pretty sure in their own minds that they can imitate anyone at all, given half a chance. And ring up any actor's agent about his client's proficiency on the football park and a close approximation of the following conversation will result:

'Archie? Play football? You're not serious, are you?'

'I'm in deadly earnest. You see I'm casting a play about a footballer and . . .'

'Archie was playing striker for his Middlesbrough Junior Stage School when he was *ten years old*.'

'Really? I didn't realize that. . . .'

'I'm telling you, dear boy. When Archie was with the Burslem Repertory Company, he not only skippered the Rep Eleven, he also played 160 games of senior amateur football in the Midland Central League.'

'If he'd like to pop along tomorrow we're auditioning at. . . .'

'Of course, you heard about the trial he had with Q.P.R.?'

'To be absolutely honest, I didn't know. . . .'

'They wanted him to turn pro. I had hell's own job getting Dave Sexton to leave this office with his contract unsigned.'

'He sounds like just the sort of chap we're . . .'

'And Arsenal. They were after him. I'm telling you, dear boy, Bertie Mee was an embarrassment, down on his bended knees. I could have done a swop. If Archie had gone to Arsenal, I could have had Peter Storey and Charlie George in the touring production of *No, No, Nanette!*'

And so forth, and so forth. . . .

Making allowances and taking the agent's eulogies with a sack of salt, you would still be excused for forming the opinion that his client was possessed with some *slight* idea of the basic rudiments of the game.

Not a bit of it.

When Archie turns up for the audition (along with a dozen or so other budding Norman Hunters), you will only too quickly discover that his interest in football is rather less than cursory. It is just possible that he once attended a matinée performance of *Zigger-Zagger* – if not and if taxed about his knowledge of the sport, he'll probably reply:

'Soccer? Ah! Mmmmm! Now let me think – is that the one with the round ball – or is it the one where they use the sausage-shaped thingy?'

Coupled with which, and as Jackie Charlton acutely observed, he won't have footballers' legs.

What he will bring to the part, however, is unbounded enthusiasm. All members of the theatrical profession are brimful of it. Enthusiasm is part and parcel of every actor's stock-in-trade.

I am reminded of one particular television play of mine when, on the first day of rehearsal, you never saw eleven more enthusiastic lads gathered together. Even the director was immediately infected by their enthusiasm.

'They might not *look* much like footballers,' he said. 'But they are enthusiastic. Give me a couple of weeks with them and you'll think they're Leeds United.'

I had some slight reservations, but I was willing to go along with him.

After only a few days of rehearsal, those boys were so keyed up you might easily have mistaken the atmosphere in that rehearsal room for that of a Wembley dressing-room on Cup Final day.

Some few days before we were due to record the play, the director organized a proper game of football for them in order to keep them at their peak. There were a lot of football plays about at the time and it was easy enough to find our lads some opposition from the ranks of their colleagues.

And so it came about that, at 10.30 on a bleak and out-of-season Wednesday morning, eleven pretend-footballers were ushered into a *real* dressing-room prior to taking part in a *real* football match, some of them for the first time in their lives.

The dressing-room contained *real* showers, and our lads were provided with a *real* football strip and *real* boots by the television props department, who had further excelled themselves by bringing along *real* oranges for refreshment at half-time. There was even *real* liniment to rub on their limbs before the start of the game.

'But, my darlings, you all look so incredibly *butch*!' squealed the gentleman from the costume department, quite taken away by the excitement of it all.

And the footballing actors chattered animatedly and enthusiastically as they prepared themselves. In no time at all, they had mastered the intricacies of tie-ups and laces and were dressed and ready for the battle ahead. It had to be admitted that they looked the part – viewed above the waist.

I had myself invited an ex-professional player along to act as referee, as well as have a good laugh, and it was his whistle that summoned both teams out on to the park.

It was at this point precisely that Life and Art failed to fuse.

Directly outside the dressing-rooms was a concrete path, no more than three feet wide, but still a hazard that had to be crossed in order to get on to the actual pitch.

Twenty-one actor–footballers managed to get across. One actor–footballer did not.

The casualty was a chap in his early thirties. He had never before played football in his life. He had never before worn football boots. He was entirely unaware of the existence of football studs.

As he ran out of the dressing-room he stamped one studded boot on the concrete path and up he went, one leg first and then the other, propelled into a full backward somersault from which he landed, inelegantly, chin first, on the concrete path.

We lifted him gently and carried him back into the dressing-room. We laid him on a bench.

If the *Guinness Book of Records* is interested, I would put him forward as the only man to be injured at football who has never actually kicked a ball.

As we waited for the ambulance to arrive, the gentleman from the costume department proved to be a real Florence Nightingale, and the injured actor–footballer was tended with a mother's loving care. He was taken to hospital, his chin was stitched, and he was returned to us in a couple of days in time to play his part in the television studio.

As for the actual game we played that raw morning, and for the record books, our side of pretend-footballers beat the other side of pretend-footballers by the odd goal in three, even though we played with a man short.

It was not a memorable match.

The players hadn't got footballers' legs.

Believe me, I am not knocking the acting profession. After all, I'm sure those lads did as well as, if not better than, Charlie George and Peter Storey would have managed in the touring production of *No, No, Nanette!*

4 TEAM TALK

From *They Don't All Open Men's Boutiques*,
B.B.C. TV, 1972

*The scene is the dressing-room of a Football League Club
that is struggling near the foot of the Fourth Division. It is
4.45 on a Saturday afternoon and the club has just lost at
home for the umpteenth time this season. The players are
sitting disconsolately around the dressing-room muddied,
bloodied, whacked out, and displaying various depths and
attitudes of dejection. Next week they face Leeds United
away in an early round of the FA Cup, and it is the task
of their manager, Wilf Hardiman, to raise the spirits of his
beaten team and convince them that they stand a cat-in-
hell's chance of achieving the impossible.*

HARDIMAN: So listen. You're the ones who've got it to
do next week. Not me. So listen. You know we've got the
big one coming up? Leeds United. (*The players stir with
interest, sit up, take notice*) At Elland Road. The FA Cup.
The road to Wembley. The twin towers beckoning, eh?
If you can beat Leeds United. All right then. But you're
the ones that have got to do it, in the final analysis. Not
me – you. So. Do you or do you not want to talk about it?
Because if you *don't* want to talk about it, I'm alla keef.
You only have to say. I'll go home. Because you're the
ones that have got it to do. So, what do you want to talk
about?

*The players exchange nervous glances, each waiting for
someone else to be the first to speak. At last,* CRUNCH, *their
rugged centre-half and captain ventures an opinion:*

CRUNCH: Well – speaking for myself, Wilf, *personally* speaking, I'd rather see another runner up front, just to run on to loose balls if nothing else.

There is a murmur of agreement.

HARDIMAN: Never mind tactics. Tactics don't interest me today. I'll worry about tactics, you leave all that to me. That's my job, tactics. Don Revie? *(He taps his forehead.)* Up here. I'll outsmart Don Revie, have no fear. What? I'll *lose* Don Revie up here. No, that's not the problem, is it? That's the last thing we have to worry about, as of now. It's more a question of attitudes, isn't it? As of now, it's a question of can you lot go out at Elland Road and do Leeds United? *(A murmur of doubt.)* Ah! Now! You see? What it is, in the final analysis, it's a question of do you *think* you can do it?

JERICHO: No chance.

HARDIMAN: What sort of a bloody attitude is that to come out with?

JERICHO: You asked for opinions, I'm telling you – no chance.

HARDIMAN *(furious)*: No, and you never will have no bloody chance, not while you go around with ideas like that in your head! No chance. Charming. Listen. *(And again he taps his forehead.)* You've got to *know* you can do it, up here. *(He points to his legs.)* Let these do the running for you. *(Striking his breast.)* This. Here. Heart Plenty of this. Bloody pride. That's all it takes. Confidence. Mental attitude, matey, and a bit of bloody human dignity, that's what wins matches. Confidence and pride and human bloody dignity and you can go out there and *slaughter* any team that God cares to send. And *I'm* telling that. Me. It's my job to get you in the right attitude, and I'm telling you. Now. I – think – you – can – get – out – on – the – park – and – take – Leeds – United. Play them off the pitch. I do. *(He throws a clenched right fist in the air.)* Crucify 'em! I sincerely believe that. The big question is, do *you* believe it?

23

Because if you don't, I'm wasting my time. *(He glances at each one of them in turn and is met by silence and down-turned eyes.)* Right then. You see my problem, don't you? I think you can beat them, you think otherwise. It's as simple as that.

CRUNCH: Could be.

HARDIMAN: But it *is* that simple. It's football, isn't it? What it all comes down to. Football. Thump or be thumped, that's all it is.

SEDGEWICK: Come off it, Wilf.

HARDIMAN: Come off what?

SEDGEWICK: It's like Crunch says, it's *not* that simple.

HARDIMAN: What is it then? Go on, you tell me.

SEDGEWICK: All kinds of things. You have to examine it from every angle. In one way, it's a question of suscepti-bilities.

JERICHO: Right.

SEDGEWICK: We're susceptible at the back and we're susceptible up front.

JERICHO: Right.

HARDIMAN: Look, son, don't you sit there and start long-wording it with me. Coming the ab-dabs with the bleedin' long words. That's not going to solve our prob-lem. Bloody long words never won nobody the FA Cup.

SEDGEWICK: You're asking for opinions. All I'm trying to do is put things in perspective, state a few pertinent facts.

CRUNCH: He's right, boss.

JERICHO: Right.

There is a general murmur of approval from the rest of the team and HARDIMAN *is forced to concede a point.*

HARDIMAN: All right, son. Carry on. You have the floor.

SEDGEWICK: I'm saying, you mentioned confidence. Right. Well. Examine statistics. How many teams this season have gone up to Elland Road and won away from home, and how many times have we gone away from home – and won?

CRUNCH: We haven't.
WILKINS: No.
Another general murmur of agreement from the other players.
HARDIMAN *waits for total silence and then points an accusing finger at* SEDGEWICK.

HARDIMAN: In the *league*.
SEDGEWICK: Well?
HARDIMAN: You're talking *league* statistics. *League* statistics don't come into it. Because we're not talking about *league* football, are we? We're talking about *cup* football. Topsy-turvy football. A different thing entirely. Also, something else I'll give you to consider: the crowd factor.
JERICHO *(mystified)*: Crowd factor?
HARDIMAN: That's it.
JERICHO: Up there? At Elland Road?
HARDIMAN: Dead right. The crowd factor. There's going to be thirty thousand plus out on them terraces next Saturday.
JERICHO: Shouting for Leeds United, yes. 'Come on, Clarky!' 'Come on, Bremner!' How does that help us?
HARDIMAN *(shouting)*: Never mind who for. Thirty thousand upraised voices, *plus*. And you tell me that isn't going to raise your game?
CRUNCH: You think it will?
HARDIMAN: I know it will. Since when did you last play in front of thirty thousand plus? And there'll be more than one of that lot our supporters, don't you fret.
JERICHO: Give over. They don't even come to watch us when we play at home. When we did last take *one* bus-load of supporters to an away game?
HARDIMAN: When did we last play Leeds United in the FA Cup? They'll be there – our lot – because they're not bad lads.
JERICHO *(bitterly)*: They're fantastic, our supporters.

We've got a great relationship. *(Glaring at* CRUNCH.*)* Ever since our skipper chinned the secretary of the Supporters' club.

CRUNCH: I'd bloody chin him again, mate, don't you fret.

JERICHO: I know you would, I don't doubt it.

CRUNCH: I'll hang one on you, too, if you give me any of your old moody.

HARDIMAN *(interceding, hastily)*: All right, all right, leave it out, lads. Listen. All I'm saying is, you're going out next Saturday afternoon in front of thirty thousand faces, plus. Right? Forget where they come from, forget who they are, forget who they're shouting for – just let them shout. That's all. *(He crosses and puts his hand on the head of a diminutive player who wears the number seven shirt and answers to the name of* ROGER*)*. When this lad starts weaving down that line, skinning Norman Hunter, you think that crowd isn't going to get up on its toes and shout for him? 'ROH-JER!' 'ROH-JER!' And you just tell me if that isn't going to lift your game? What did it do to Colchester? What did Colchester do to Leeds United in a previous FA Cup?

ROGER, *who was beginning to go along with* HARDIMAN, *has sudden doubts.*

ROGER: What did Colchester do to us though, in that pre-season friendly?

HARDIMAN: For crying out loud, lad. Look back on your triumphs. Why drag up past tragedies? It's what it's all about, isn't it? Frame of mind. The right frame of mind this afternoon and you'd have gone out there and *won!* Won. Beat them, instead of getting beat. Same as the right frame of mind next Saturday and you can go up there and work the miracle. What am I saying, 'miracle'? It's been done before. They're not unbeatable. They're only players. They're not bleedin' gods, you know. Clog them, they'll feel it. Stripe them, they'll bleed. Put that ball in their net and their heads will drop. Eleven players, that's all they are – the same as you. One substitute. Go through the card, study the team-sheets, man for man – you can take them.

CRUNCH: Leeds United?

HARDIMAN: Yes.

CRUNCH: *Beat* them? We can?

HARDIMAN: Certainly. No trouble. If you *believe* you can. Belief. Moves mountains, eh? *(He displays an upturned clenched fist.)* And this. Plenty of this. Go. Yes. You can beat them. *Bloody yes!*

And HARDIMAN's *power of oratory has succeeded at least in convincing himself.*

5 HOW MY STYLE WAS CRAMPED

Football first struck me as being a hazardous pursuit prior to a street football match many, many years ago when an infant centre-forward, one little Ronnie Reynard by name, swallowed the ha'penny with which we were about to toss up. Ronnie's resultant piercing screams ensured that the rest of us players were dragged off home by our respective parents, and that particular football match was struck from the fixture list.

Ronnie himself was lugged off to Leeds General Infirmary where he dined off cotton-wool sandwiches, needlessly it transpired, for the ha'penny (which turned out to be Irish anyway) found a way out of its own accord before the treatment had time to work.

Ultimately, Ronnie was the only one to come out of the episode the better off – he was allowed to keep the coin as a souvenir, unfairly, I have always thought, for I have always maintained that the coin came out of my pocket.

Yes, I have always recognized football as an injurious sport – particularly to me, for I am injury prone.

For example, from the first moment that I stood up proudly on two legs and walked, right up until the day that I was put into long trousers, I cannot remember that a day went by when I wasn't suffering from a scabby knee (perm any leg from two).

Not that it worried me overmuch, but I seem to remember that it gave my mother a great deal of cause for concern. 'Footballing again,' I can hear her sigh. 'Just look at him, he's not fit to be taken anywhere! I wanted to take him to have his photograph done on Saturday, but just look at his scabby knees!'

'Have him done head and shoulders,' suggested my father.

An obvious solution, and I still have that very studio portrait to this day – me at the age of six in a green cap with yellow piping and a green jersey with a wolf-cub motif. I am standing awkwardly in the photograph, my hands held rigidly by my sides, my legs cut off just above the knees. You would have thought that the Leeds studio photographer would have devised a more natural way of posing a scabby-kneed lad, for Lord knows I was not the only one.

Scabby knees were the lot of all boy footballers in those days. Boy cricketers suffered from broken front teeth and disjointed fingers, but boy footballers were instantly recognizable by their scabby knees. It was mostly because of the rough-and-ready pitches we played on.

I once played as striker for Scotland in a gruelling international when we lost, unluckily I have always thought, to England by 135 goals to 3. I was eight years old then, and that particular international fixture was played out in a cobbled outside-lavvy yard and was played with a mangy tennis-ball, with chalk-marks serving for goal-posts. The disparity in the score-line was caused partly by the fact that I didn't *want* to play for Scotland anyway, but was mostly down to the four boundary walls of the pitch which were built of solid brick.

Not to beat about the bush, I am an out-and-out born coward, and being shouldered roughly on to brick closet walls, jarring bone and grazing skin, was never my idea of an afternoon's sport.

Indeed, England's goal tally that afternoon (take note Mr Revie) might have been much higher, had not the match been abandoned before full time when a local adult resident had recourse to put the lavvy yard to its proper use and therefore chucked us infant-internationals out.

I was reminded of that historic fixture the other day when I read somewhere that certain members of the Professional Footballers' Association had registered strong objections at the prospect of being invited to earn their daily bread on various forms of artificial turf.

'I can't say I blame them,' muttered Old Man Memory at my ear, as he settled easily into a comfortable position, the reins in his hand, and careered of on yet another trip down his favourite lane. . . .

Oh yes, I have played on more than one peculiar football ground in my day. And I can state, categorically and contrary to popular opinion, that there is nothing new about artificial turf. *I* was playing on artificial football pitches as a schoolboy player some thirty-odd long years ago. Not that I ever played on anything which in any way approximated to a close facsimile of actual *turf*.

In those dim and distant days, in the north of England at least, we bloodied our knees, elbows, and any portions of our anatomy that protruded from our clothing, on

artificial playing fields that went under the name of cinder pitches.

If nothing else, they were well-named, for that was exactly what they were: areas of rock-hard ground that had been liberally bestrewn with sharp black cinders. These patches of black wasteland, looking like flattened slag-heaps, were then marked out as football pitches and had goalposts (*sans* nets) stuck up at either end. And on these cinder pitches Yorkshire schoolboy football was kept alive – nay, flourished – *circa* 1937. In fact, cinder pitches were so much the norm that I think I must have been all of nine or ten years old before I realized that football was *intended* to be played on grass.

Not that there was any shortage of real grass in those days, curiously enough. The cinder-pitches themselves were almost always to be found in parks or on public open spaces where neatly mowed grassland abounded on all four sides – a sea of grass, no less, surrounding every cinder-pitch. But in the thirties, the adamant municipal rule was DO NOT WALK ON THE GRASS, and so to play football on it was unthinkable.

We played on cinder pitches, and we suffered from scabby knees. Either that or we played cricket on those same cinders and the ball came off them awkwardly and we broke our front teeth or mutilated our fingers. As I have already pointed out, I am a natural coward and so I gave up competitive sport in my early teens until I was able to enjoy the luxury of thick grass pitches in my army days.

I took up rugby in the army, and I turned my back on playing soccer until I was all of thirty-seven years old, when I was invited to turn out for a celebrity team.

I bought myself real soccer boots for the first time (I had never actually *owned* a pair as a boy) and a jock-strap and shin-pads, and I purloined a bath-towel emblazoned with the name of a first division club, I bought myself an Adidas bag to contain my sporting clothes.

The first game I turned out in was a friendly game that

was played inside one of Her Majesty's Prisons when we took on the inmates' team. With deep pride, I can define our front line-up on that occasion as the Three Aitches: Hill (Jimmy), Haynes (Johnny) and Hall (Me).

And what lush green turf we played on in that nick! None of your cruel knee-biting cinder-pitches in these cosseted times, not even for the criminal classes.

But, as I have already pointed out, I am injury prone. Injury struck, alas, some ten minutes after the kick-off when I went down with chronic cramp – in both legs at the same time. I lay for a time on the pitch, while the game continued, flat on my back but with both of my lower limbs sticking straight up in the air, rather like a dead pigeon. I was carried from the field by four men, with my body and legs at an exact angle of ninety degrees. I was in agony.

Johnny Haynes had to be assisted from the pitch a few minutes later. He was also suffering from cramp, although his was situated in the stomach and had been caused by laughing at me.

I don't play much football these days, there isn't much incentive. There is little in the way of kudos left to hope for. I see small chance of my being selected for England now that I am forty-five – it's not only my age that's against me, there's also the fact that I've already represented Scotland in the lavvy yard fiasco, for Sir Alf must surely take that into account whenever he selects his squad.

Anyway, I have come to the opinion that there can't be much of a future career in soccer for a forty-five year old coward who is injury prone. I'm thinking very seriously indeed about selling my boots, if anybody's interested:

'*Size nine, one owner, very low mileage. . . .*'

6 THERE'S NO BUSINESS . . .

From *Sportsworld*, 1974

There is, I have been solemnly assured on good authority, a well-known member of the acting profession who now attends all of his rehearsals wearing a Leeds track-suit. Well, I for one have no reason to doubt it. I have myself enjoyed the singular experience of bumping into another actor, some months ago, walking along Brighton seafront and got up in a Chelsea number nine shirt.

'Hallo there, Willis!' he greeted me cheerily with upraised blue-sleeved arm and clenched fist.

We chatted for a while of work and of absent friends and of other inconsequentialities until, unable to contain my puzzlement any longer, I ventured: 'Excuse me, but would you mind telling me why you are taking the air in a Chelsea number nine shirt?'

'It's Peter Osgood's,' said the well-known actor, as if that was reason and justification enough.

Well, it takes all sorts to make a world.

I have yet to hear of a training session at Elland Road when Billy Bremner has trotted on to the pitch togged out as Charley's Aunt – nor do I know of a kiddies birthday party where Peter Osgood has turned up as entertainer, with a suitcase full of conjuring tricks in one hand and a Sooty glove on the other – but give it time, give it time. . . .

The uneasy alliance between the theatrical profession and the world of soccer continues apace, albeit with shifting values.

In the good old days, of course, it was Tommy Trinder making jokes about his chairmanship at Fulham, and that was it – but in the sports-conscious times we live in, it seems that everybody wants to get into the act.

Witness the appearance – or should one say performance? – of Raquel Welch at Stamford Bridge in 1973.

'I wonder how many of you knew,' enthused Jimmy Hill, then with London Weekend Television, *'that Raquel Welch was a fervent Chelsea supporter?'*

I have to hand it to you, Jim old lad, and thank you for putting us in the picture, not many of us did. And I suspect that Miss Welch herself didn't know much about it either, until she was informed of her allegiance by her publicity agent. But credit the lady with acting ability, for she certainly had a lot of people fooled, including: soccer's leading analyst and linesman; the whole of the Chelsea team; London Weekend Television's Sports Department; the Chelsea board of directors – everyone, it seems, except the viewing public when LWT misjudged its audience's intelligence and screened the greatest sporting camera-hugging exhibition since Hitler stuck his nose in at the 1936 Olympics.

But then, Stamford Bridge has long been the favourite stamping ground for itinerant members of the acting world. A few years ago, it was reckoned close enough to Craven Cottage for actors to switch their loyalty to whichever of the two was the most successful club at the time. But since Fulham seem to have settled, temporarily at least, for the Second Division, most of the Thespians have burnt their bridges, bought season tickets at Chelsea, and chosen to stick to First Division status for as long as it lasts. And now they parade themselves at all home fixtures, minnying around in their sheepskin overcoats, gracing the air with after-shave, signing autograph books with panache and bumming half-time tea-room tickets without it. On occasion, there are so many members of the theatrical profession crowded into the Chelsea stand that the referee would be well-advised to dispense with his whistle and control the game with cries of *'Action!'*

and '*Cut!*', in order to ensure the maximum of crowd participation.

Not *all* football-minded actors go to Chelsea, of course. To draw a sort of idiot general rule of thumb: most actors who play middle-class parts go to Chelsea; most actors who play working-class parts go to West Ham; and members of the Light Entertainment branch of the business (Disc Jockeys included) mostly seem to favour Arsenal. There is even an élite coterie of London's theatrical family that remains steadfastly loyal to Hull City – a sad group of homesick actors still joined to their parent city by a kind of Humberical cord, if you'll pardon the pun – but there lies a story in itself.

And before we start exploring the division's of Show-business' soccer allegiance, it would be interesting to examine *why* its members go to football in the first place. For while some of them were born to it, others were not, and plainly not all of them understand or even enjoy the game, and certainly only those that *have* succeeded in bumming half-time tea-room tickets are happy during the half-time break – the ones that haven't got tickets get

to their feet, shuffle about, flash about, flash their best profile to the terraces, pray to God that they'll be recognized, and then pretend they haven't noticed if they are.

Again, *why* do they do it?

For it is fairly safe to state that these days football grounds are the only places where actors choose to mingle with the general public – that's with the exception of charitable functions, political demonstrations, and the annual fair on Hampstead Heath. Ordinarily, actors prefer to keep themselves to themselves. They have their own exclusive clubs, they stick rigidly to their own restaurants – and although they may occasionally slip into a theatre in the evenings, they hardly ever go into a cinema at night, preferring the relative obscurity of matinées. So why do they choose, on one day a week, to toss themselves in at the deep-end so to speak, with anything from ten to forty thousand of the hoi polloi?

Being fashionable is mostly what it's all about. And as long as football *is* fashionable, then the acting profession will remain relentlessly loyal to the game.

There was a time, some ten or twelve years ago, when footballers courted the attentions of Showbusiness. Those soccer players who were lucky enough to count members of the world of entertainment among their friends were fêted in flash restaurant-clubs where they sat, goggle-eyed and awkwardly clutching at long-stemmed wine-glasses, gazing at the stars of stage, screen and television that languidly decorated near-by tables.

These days the boot is laced up firmly on the other foot, and it's the entertainment world that gawps in awe at footballers who hog both limelight and coveted corner-tables. Some of the players now even make so bold as to take their courage and the menu in both hands and eschew the previously obligatory footballer's order of '*Steak and chips miss, please, well done*', in favour of Saddle of Lamb or Roast Rib Beef, although not many of them as yet will tackle a menu that is couched in any sort of alien language.

A few football managers have recently discovered champagne – although they never denied its previous existence, it had always been recognized as some sort of shampoo that was poured over players' heads after good results in cup-ties – and now swig it back as if it was going out of style. Those self-same rough-hewn managers of simple tastes who, it seemed, had forsaken tobacco long years since when they put their names to their apprentice forms, now strut around with their jaws clamped on cigars so big they would make Sir Lew Grade cower.

Where will it all end, one wonders?

Even now, the entertainment world is making wider inroads into soccer's boardrooms: Eric Morecambe at Luton Town, Richard Attenborough at Stamford Bridge, Elton John at Watford. And, lower down the football echelons, among the amateurs in the Rothman's Isthmian League, there's Alan Simpson beavering away at Hampton Football Club.

So where *do* we go from here?

Will Rodney Marsh eventually get an Oscar for his celebrated performances in *The Box*? Shall we see Alf Garnett have his name taken for the constant use of bad language *on* the box? Should actors selected for the National Theatre company be awarded England caps? Is there any truth in the rumour that Steve McQueen is buying Leeds United for Ali McGraw's birthday? Will Val Parnell enter into a transfer deal with Don Revie for Norman Hunter, offering him £200,000 and Gary Glitter in part exchange? Will Des O'Connor ever play for Arsenal? And before you snigger at that last one, Des O'Connor *was*, at one time, actually on Northampton Town's books as a Youth Team player.

And then what?

Are we headed towards some awful hybrid form of sport and theatre, where the players exchange jock-straps for cod-pieces and club colours for sequinned leotards?

Is there nothing constant in the game of football? Is

there nothing changeless left to grasp hold of in this ever-changing world?

Very, very little, I'm afraid to say.

Well, there is Bill Shankly's thirst for lemonade, for one thing. And then there's his hairstyle, for another. And thank God for them both. For if we ever catch Mr Shankly with a champagne cocktail in his hand, or with his hair-line creeping anywhere near his collar – we can all start to sweat in earnest.

7 CHILD'S PLAY

The hopes that I carried for my son's future as a sporting giant took another severe jolt last week when he set off for school carrying a large gold-and-off-white teddy bear. He is now coming up for seven, an age when I had expected him to go striding away each morning with a pair of dinky soccer boots slung round his neck, or lugging his own miniature cricket bag.

Furthermore, he carried the teddy-bear without embarrassment and without benefit of plain cover or carrier bag. His claim that his Junior Mixed Infants School was holding a Teddy-Bear Week seemed scant excuse, and served only to strengthen my doubts about modern education.

Surely, at coming up for seven, Tom Brown was playing wing-threequarter for Rugby's second XV – to say nothing of being held over fires as part of a rigid toughening-up process? Even in these namby-pamby modern days, if I am to believe my *Sunday Times*, Michael Parkinson has a whole host of sturdy lads who tuck home goals and know exactly where silly-mid-off is situated. Where did it all go wrong, I begin to wonder?

I set the lad off on the right foot, surely to Malcolm Allison? I obtained the services of an ex-England soccer captain as his godfather. I obtained permission from a leading National Hunt jockey to name the boy after him. I should explain, perhaps, that for many years I have cherished a fantasy in which I father a boy who rushes off the Wembley turf, having captained Leeds United to FA Cup victory, nips into a waiting helicopter, and skies away to ride home the 33–1 outsider in the last race at

Kempton. In my fantasy, the boy winks at his grizzled father on his way out of the paddock to the starting gates 'Try me for a fiver each way, old 'un!' Thus had I dreamed of being kept in my old age.

Again, I ask myself, where did it all go wrong? To begin with, my aspirations for the lad's racing career took a steep nosedive when he began to experience serious problems with his racing weight at the age of two-and-a-half. On top of which, his soccer future began to look less than rosy when the very sight of a pumped-up football was enough to send him into screaming tantrums.

When the boy was three, I put up a set of junior goal-posts in the garden in the hope of egging him along. Then, as he seemed to have no talent whatsoever for kicking the ball with either foot, let alone both, I engaged the help of a friendly ex-Fulham goalkeeper who agreed to come round regularly, for old times' sake, and give him lessons between the sticks. The friendly ex-Fulham goal-keeper, being a good chum of the ex-England captain godfather to the boy, was full of enthusiasm at first, but gave up entirely half-way through the second session. My son, it seemed had a rare gift for diving out of the way of the approaching ball.

'I'm afraid he just hasn't got it, Willis,' sighed my friendly ex-Fulham goalkeeper, and I have not set eyes on him from that day to this.

Not that I was deterred by early setbacks – and as witness to the fact, my cellar and summerhouse are both knee-high in various discarded sporting equipments in midget sizes: tiny tennis rackets plus balls and net; a half-set of golf clubs cut down to size; almost all of a kiddies cricket outfit; shuttlecocks galore. There is even a miniature base-ball bat, glove and Los Angeles Dodgers' cap, gifts from a kindly itinerant Hollywood restaurateur. My garden resembles an Olympic training ground for dwarfs.

My son not only ignores this panoply of sporting

opportunity – he will not even venture out of doors into God's good air except under threat of physical torture.

When he arrived at the ripe old age of six, I was ready to admit defeat. After all, I am informed on very good authority that Australian swimming champions are chucked into the deep end at the age of two, muck or nettles. He had turned down my offer for his birthday of a punchball and a rowing machine and had opted instead for an encyclopedia of prehistoric animals and a matched set of coloured felt tip pens. And it was at this point that my mind began to think in other directions. Perhaps I was being too harsh on him? For what was there in my own past sporting history for him to hook his personal star on? My four or five appearances as scrum-half for the Royal Signals Far East Land Forces (Singapore) Rugby XV, plus a few seasons spent in the obscurity of Sunday morning soccer, hardly qualified me for the Sportsman of the Year Award. And, if the lad did take after me, then why not capitalize on it? The pen is mightier than the vaulting pole, at least it is as far as raking in the shekels goes.

I made a decision. If my boy was just not cut out to be a Billy Bremner or a Norman Hunter or an Eddie Gray – then why shouldn't he become a Hugh McIlvanney or a Geoffrey Green or a John Moynihan? I immediately experienced a new and most enjoyable fantasy:

'Hello, old 'un! Sorry to ring you at this time of night, but I've got a couple of tickets going spare in the press-box for tomorrow's final. I'll leave them at the ticket-office in our name.'

Not at all a bad parental fantasy – for starters. But if dream was to become reality, I would have to backtrack slightly. I had got his back up about sport, and I would have to kindle in him a new love for it. I decided upon a fatherly chat to begin with.

'Look here, son, if you've definitely decided against participating in competitive sport. . . .' His eyes lit up. I was off to a good start. 'I honestly don't mind,' I continued, 'if you've *definitely* decided – but if you aren't going to join in yourself, why not start watching other people playing?'

'Why?' He found the idea novel, if not intriguing.

'Well. . . .' I was patience itself. 'Well, lots of lads who don't actually *play*, go along and watch their favourite team on Saturday afternoons. Or, if they can't actually go, they read about them and they get their autographs and they watch them on the telly. They're called fans. You've seen them standing on the terraces in *The Big Match* on Sunday afternoons.' He seemed unsure, and so I added for clarification: 'It comes on after *Thunderbirds*.'

'Oh, yes.' His brow cleared.

'So how about it?'

'What do I have to do?'

'Choose a team. Any team. And follow it.'

The above keen and intelligent sporting discussion was followed by a three-day pause after which he came up to me off his own bat and announced:

'I'm Liverpool.'

'Good! Great!' I enthused. 'You'll like that. There's Kevin Keegan and Stevie Heighway and lots of other clever players – you can cut their pictures out of magazines and stick them in a book. And we'll look in the paper together every Saturday night and see how they've got on.'

Suddenly, it seemed, a great weight had been lifted from my shoulder – had some of it come to rest, I wondered, upon the able and capable shoulders of Bill Shankly? I hoped so, for I had every faith in the man. I bought my boy a button-hole badge and, the very next day, he set out for school displaying it bravely.

He came home without it.

'What's happened to your Liverpool badge?'

I discovered he had swopped it for a two inch model of a stegosaurus that came from out of a corn flake packet.

'What did you do that for?'

'I'm not Liverpool any longer.'

'Why not?' I tried to keep calm. I told myself that, after all, the stegosaurus had been on this earth for millions of years before Kevin Keegan was ever thought of.

'Because Harold Bullock, in my class, says Liverpool are crackers.'

'Well, Mr Shankly doesn't think so. He's *proud* of Liverpool. And what about Stevie Heighway and all the others?'

'I don't know,' he shrugged. 'Anyway I'm not Liverpool any longer. I'm Leeds United.'

A light shone in the darkness. I couldn't fault the lad, I have been a Leeds United supporter all my life. I bequeathed my son a buttonhole badge of my own and, to be fair to the boy, he wore it regularly.

A couple of months ago I took him to see his first full ninety minutes of football. Not Leeds United, for we live in the south of England, but the local amateur team. We stood on the terraces together, father and son, along with a couple of hundred other stalwarts. The boy watched the game for several minutes, then ventured:

'Which one's Leeds United?'

'Neither. The ones in the blue-and-gold are St Albans, and the ones in the white are Dulwich Hamlet.'

The answer didn't surprise him or displease him, in fact he showed no interest in my reply. Some few minutes later he drifted away from the terraces and spent the remainder of the first forty-five minutes throwing Coca-Cola bottle tops at the park railings. When I looked for him at half-time he had gone home. He has never mentioned St Albans City, Dulwich Hamlet or even Leeds United again.

So where *did* I go wrong?

The lad comes from sturdy Yorkshire stock. Is there none of that county fire in his veins similar to that which courses through the veins of Freddie Trueman or Roger Taylor or Harvey Smith?

No – none. Well, perhaps there is still hope.

Last Friday, at the end of Teddy Bear Week at his Junior Mixed Infants School, my son came home lugging back his gold-and-off-white teddy bear. The bear was sporting a rosette, having been awarded, it read, 'Third Prize for Cheekiest Teddy.' Did I detect a faint glimmer of triumph in the lad's eyes? I think I did, I certainly think I did.

Next year at this time he will be coming up for eight, and what then? 'Second Prize for Best Dressed Teddy'? And what about the year after that, when he will be almost nine? 'First Prize for Best Teddy Overall'! It's possible.

Yes, there is hope still. We are not by any means defeated. So look out, you would-be Olympians for 1984. We Halls are notorious slow-starters, but when the chips are down . . .

8 ANOTHER CHRISTMAS CAROL

It had been one of the more affluent of football dinners. I had dined on lobster cocktail and peppered steak, the wine and the brandy had flowed freely and, consequently, I was not in the least surprised to see the apparition by my bedside at two o'clock in the morning.

'Who are you, Spirit?' I demanded of it, slightly bemused at finding myself not in the least afraid.

'I am the Ghost-of-Football-Past,' he sighed. For added effect he rattled his chain, which seemed to be fashioned out of FA Cup runners-up medals.

'What is it that you want of me?' My question was superfluous, for I knew my Dickens – I had seen the film. Even before the Spirit's reply, I was clutching at his sleeve and my eyes were shut tight, anticipating the experience to come. I was not disappointed. The rush of cold air told me that we had gone out through the open window and were travelling fast through time and space.

We stopped. My feet touched ground.

'Open your eyes,' demanded my ghostly companion, 'and tell me what you see.'

We were standing outside a working-class terraced house, and I judged by the street gas-lamp standards that we were in the north of England in the thirties. Looking through the window outside which we had put down, I saw a young lad with a pudding-basin crop and a green Wolf Cub jersey unwrapping his Christmas presents. He produced a pair of pre-war football boots and examined them excitedly. They were dung-coloured, bulbous-toed and high-ankled, as if intended for some surgical purpose. I recognized the boots before I recognized the boy.

'Those were my boots,' I cried. 'That's me. I was eight years old and I was going to grow up to be the centre forward for Leeds United and gain representative honours with England.'

'And did you?' asked the Spirit.

'No,' I admitted.

'Why was that?'

'As things turned out,' I said, 'I was never much good at playing football.'

'Close your eyes,' bade my Spirit guide, 'and catch at my sleeve.'

Again, I did as I was told and, once more, we whirled off. This time our trip was short.

When I opened my eyes we were looking in at the window of what I took to be a workman's cottage. The simple workman and his family were grouped around a scrubbed deal table on which there stood a small repast: the remains of a chicken, some cold Christmas pudding, a half-empty bowl of custard, a half-bottle of cheap port wine. I guessed that we had journeyed backward in time some few years and that this was Boxing Day. I was right. I further hazarded that the man was a lowly farm labourer. I was wrong.

'He *is* the centre forward for Leeds United,' said the Spirit.

'But where is his fast car?' I queried. 'Or even his garage? Indeed, where is his mock-Georgian residence with its billiards room? Where are his wall-to-wall carpets and his picture windows and where is his well-stocked fitted bar?'

'I am the Ghost-of-Football-Past,' the Spirit reminded me.

Even so, I found his assertation difficult to believe.

'Stay, Spirit!' I cried. 'If he *is* the Leeds United centre forward, and if it really *is* Boxing Day —'

'He is and it is,' the apparition intoned.

'Then surely he would be playing football this very afternoon? A league fixture. That man is not in a fit condition to turn out for a pea-pushing competition, let alone a football match. He's full of warm ale and cold pudding.'

'In those days,' said the Spirit, 'at Christmastime, the players often were. But he'll be on the field all right.'

'In that condition – no wonder they got less than a tenner a week!' I cried.

'Much less,' said the Spirit.

'Going out on to a field, bursting at the gut and sozzled to boot! They had no sense of priorities.'

'Perhaps not,' sighed the Spirit. 'But they cared about Christmas, they cared for their families. In my day, remember, football was just a game. Close your eyes and go back to sleep.'

I dozed fitfully until three o'clock and then I woke to find the second of the spectral visitors hovering at my bedside. This one affected a chain that rustled rather than clanked, and I guessed that it was fashioned out of referees' report forms.

'The Ghost-of-Football-Present?' I asked of it.

The Spirit nodded and, dutifully, I closed my eyes and clutched at its winding sheet.

Our journey seemed to take less than a second.

We were looking in at the window of a luxury flat. A giant of a man in his middle twenties was chewing almonds out of a silver bonbon dish while a girl in her late teens, wearing nothing but a bra and lacy knickers, ironed away at more frothy underwear.

'Where have you brought me, Spirit?' I inquired. 'Who are these people and what do we want of them?'

'This is Christmas Day 1973. Surely you recognize the man? He is one of soccer's newest and brightest Superstars.'

'Which one? Who does he play for? What are his particular skills? Can he go through the entire opposition on his own? Is he an immaculate first-time distributor of the ball? A tireless and loyal one-club worker, perhaps, who will run and run and run for his side until he drops?

Or maybe he is a goal-hungry wraith who pops up out of nowhere when he scores?'

'He is none of those,' said the Spirit. 'But he has the ability to kick everything above the ground that moves.'

'So *that's* who he is. No wonder I didn't recognize him instantly – there are a lot of them about. But if this is Christmas Day, where's his Christmas dinner?'

'He's nibbling at it now.'

'Almonds? *Nuts*? Is that it? Is that *all*?'

'He's on a very strict diet. His weight. And even if he wasn't,' said the Spirit, 'he'd still be struggling – the girl can't cook.'

'But where's his bonny homely wife, the one who does TV commercials in her kitchen? And where are those jolly rosy-cheeked children that he poses with on the covers of knitting patterns?'

'He's given them the elbow. The bird's his latest fiancée. He met her in London's newest and brightest discotheque – it's very popular with all the new bright soccer Superstars.'

I got the distinct impression suddenly that my spectral host was lapsing into very un-spectral jargon, but I decided to let it pass.

'Is he happy?' I asked.

'He's earning all of fifteen thou' a year.'

'Just for kicking everything above the ground that moves?'

'There are subsidiary perks.'

'But is he *happy*?' I persisted. 'Does he *enjoy* that kind of football?'

'Does anybody?' said the Spirit, sadly. 'Catch hold of my sleeve and close your eyes.'

The Third Spirit arrived just before dawn: a dark and morose creature lugging a heavy chain made out of light-ale bottles and bovver boots.

'Are you the Ghost-of-Football-Yet-to-Come?'

The awful spectre made no reply, save for extending his skinny, shrouded arm. I closed my eyes, grasped at skeletal bone, and was whirled off into darkness for the third time.

'Open your eyes,' commanded the Spirit.

We were standing outside a tall block of flats.

'Which window do you wish me to look through, Spirit?'

'You are not here to look through windows. Simply take note of the building.'

'Why? And what has a block of high-rise flats got to do with football?'

'The block of flats stands on the very ground where once there stood a Football League club.'

'Which Football League club?' I asked, anxiously. 'And what's happened to it? Where is it now?'

'It makes no difference which one it was,' sighed the Spirit. 'They are all of them gone to dust.'

'*Gone*? Gone how? Gone when? Gone why? And where do men play football now?'

'They don't. Not any longer. Football is as dead as . . . as Marley's ghost.'

'Why?' A cold shiver ran through me. '*Why*, Spirit, tell me why?'

'Don't you *know* why?' said the Spirit, fixing me with a sad and sorry eye.

'Because football became a game of kicking everything that moved above the ground? Because the referee's word ceased to be law?'

'That – partly.'

'It became a dull, defensive, boring pursuit, lacking in lustre and in goals, and because of that people stopped going to watch it being played?'

'That too.'

'Because violence on the field bred violence on the terraces, and men of authority who should have known better shrugged their shoulders and blamed it on a violent world?'

'That too.'

'Because football clubs persisted in treating fans like

animals and herding them in pens, and therefore the fans behaved like animals and the violence grew?'

'That too.'

'Because ordinary men became ashamed to take their wives to football grounds, and afraid to let their children go alone?'

'That too.'

'And tell me, Spirit, when was the beginning of the end?'

The Spirit gazed at me, reproachfully, and time passed before he spoke: 'Don't you already know that too?' With that, the Spirit began to fade and disappear.

'Wait, Spirit!' I cried out to him. 'Stay. One question more. Where are we standing now? Where was this place? Was it . . .' I ventured, fearfully, 'was it Elland Road?'

But the Ghost-of-Football-Yet-to-Come had gone for ever.

I set to, scrabbling at the brickwork of those flats, regardless of flesh or fingernail, as if to pull them down with my bare hands.

I awoke, true to tradition, tearing at my pillow. Was it all a dream, I wondered? And if not a dream, was it too late already – or was there hope?

Crossing to my window, I discovered half a dozen lads playing football in the street outside with a plastic ball. I called down to the smallest boy.

'Hey! You there! You, boy!'

'Whajerwant?'

'Do you know the sports shop in the High Street? The one with the match-ball in the window?'

'Course I do!'

'Then take this,' I cried, flinging a tenner down. 'And buy yourselves that ball.'

'For *us*?'

'Yes, yes, lad! You and your chums. And all I ask in return is that you play the game with it fairly, according to the rules. Practise your individual skills, never retaliate no matter how severe the foul, honour the opposition and – above all – respect the referee.'

The urchin gazed up at me, digesting my words. His young face wrinkled. Then, turning to his companions, he called: 'He's off his bleedin' rocker!' He turned his face to look up at me. 'Get stuffed!' he shouted. And the lad and his playfellows ran away.

I sighed and turned my thoughts to breakfast, dismissing the dream. I think the third Spirit was right, anyway – it is already *much* too late.

9 PUB SPORTS

From *The Piano-Smashers of the Golden Sun,*
A.T.V. 1974

PERCY CUBITT, *the sixty-five-year-old publican of The
Golden Sun and three of his regulars,* MICHAEL, CHARLES
and COLIN, *are drinking, after-hours, on a Sunday afternoon and considering ways and means of celebrating the
erection of a large block of flats outside the pub – and the
influx of trade the flats will bring in. The barmaid,* VERA,
is also present.

MICHAEL: A piano-smashing comp.
PERCY: Eh?
MICHAEL: We'll have a piano-smashing competition.
PERCY: We won't, you know, it's after three o'clock.
We're having one last drink and then we're off home.
MICHAEL: Not today, Percy. I mean for the celebrations.
For the starting of the new flats.
CHARLES: That's not a bad idea – I saw one of them
once, up at the Stag's Head.
PERCY: What's a piano-smashing competition when it's
at home?
CHARLES: It's dead simple. You have two teams from
two pubs, and they have to smash these two pianos, and
then they put the pieces through this karsey seat.
PERCY: It sounds very complicated to me.
CHARLES: It's dead simple, Percy.
PERCY: Mebbe so. But there's no bloody pianos going
down my bog, matey. I've enough problems with that
outside loo without you lot stuffing pianos down it.

VERA: Not *your* loo, Percy. They have these toilet seats hanging up on a rope, because our Cyril took me to see one last year.

CHARLES: It was at the Stag's Head. You tell him, Michael – explain.

MICHAEL: You have two teams. From two separate pubs. Are you with me so far?

PERCY: Two pubs, two teams, it's as clear as mud.

MICHAEL: Three men each team, big brawny fellers they need to be, like Colin here. And both teams have an old, clapped out piano. Like that one there.

MICHAEL *has indicated the pub piano.*

PERCY: Don't talk wet, man. That's a precision-built musical instrument. There's fifteen quid's worth of good piano there. It's got a golden tone. That's no clapped-out piano, my friend.

MICHAEL: You have three men, two sledge-hammers to a team.

PERCY: Three men, two sledges – what's the third man do?

COLIN: He spits on the hands of the other two. (*To* MICHAEL.) Sorry.

MICHAEL: You hang a rope up, right? You tie it across the yard and you hang two lavvy seats on it.

CHARLES: Your two men with the hammers, they smash the piano into little tiny pieces.

MICHAEL: And the third man stuffs the pieces through the lavvy seat.

PERCY: Why?

MICHAEL: Because it says so in the bloody rules. And the team that's first with its pieces through its karsey seat is declared the winners. (*Pause.*) So what do you say?

PERCY: It's not much of a contest, is it? Bashing a piano up? There's no – what you might call, finesse – all brawn, no brain.

MICHAEL: There's strength required, yes. But brain-work does come into it.

PERCY: Doing what? Smashing up the piano, or cramming the pieces down the loo?

COLIN: Hey! I've had a great idea! Why don't we organize a football match?

CHARLES: All four of us? We'll play the one-two-one formation and let Vera run on with the wet sponge.

COLIN: Let's challenge another pub at darts, then?

MICHAEL: What pub? With who? You're hopeless and it takes Charles two hours to get a double to throw off.

CHARLES: How about an all-comers dominoes match?

MICHAEL: Highly exciting. They'll converge on here from miles around to watch Percy lay a double-blank. No – the piano-smashing competition would be ideal.

PERCY: Except that we're not having it.

MICHAEL: Think of the business it would bring you. We challenge the Stag's Head, we know they've got a team – they'd fetch a bus-load of supporters with them, the Stag's Head.

COLIN: Can you see them Stag's Head drinkers giving up their five-way pay-out fruit machines and their infra-red steak sandwiches to tool out to a spit-and-sawdust pub like this?

PERCY: Less of your spit-and-sawdust. I'm the one that keeps this place spotless. I had to go round this morning, clearing up the muck you left behind last night.

COLIN: That's just what I'm saying, Percy – it's a mucky pub. They wouldn't want to know this pub, the Stag's Head lot.

PERCY *(glancing up at the ceiling)*: Did you hear that? *They all look up at the ceiling and listen.* PERCY'*s* WIFE *is banging with a broom on the floor above.* PERCY *opens the door and calls up the stairs.*

PERCY: Will you stop banging on that ceiling when I've got customers in! I'm trying to run a business if you did but know it! *(He turns to the men in the bar.)* Will you excuse me for one brief moment?

PERCY *bounds up the stairs.* MICHAEL, COLIN *and* CHARLES *are amused.*

COLIN: Domestic bliss.

VERA: Men – you're all alike!

MICHAEL *(reflectively)*: We'd have had some fun with a piano-smashing comp. We'd have livened this place up. You just stood there, Charles. You could have backed me up.

CHARLES: What for? We couldn't raise a team, could we? Who is there that comes in here that could swing a sledge?

MICHAEL: Colin for one.

CHARLES: Colin for one, now name another.

VERA: There's Michael or you, Charles, isn't there?

CHARLES: Swing a sledge-hammer? I couldn't swing a cat round in an aircraft hangar. Neither could he.

MICHAEL: I saw myself pushing the pieces through the lavvy seat.

COLIN: I could have asked around at work. I could have found somebody.

MICHAEL: It wouldn't have been the same though, would it? Charles is right.

COLIN: It wouldn't have been the same as what?

MICHAEL: If we'd have run a piano-smashing team, it would have had to have been a team *from* The Golden Sun. A team of Golden Sun drinkers.

CHARLES: There are none of them left, Michael, except us that's here. Not since they pulled the houses down.

COLIN: We could challenge another pub at darts, like I suggested hours since.

MICHAEL: I'm on my way to challenge my Sunday dinner. *(He drains his glass.)* And that's me finished.

VERA: Is there any chance of me begging a lift?

MICHAEL: There is if you're not going to be too long before you're ready – yes.

VERA: I'm ready now. I've only got to slip my coat on.

VERA *is putting her coat on as* PERCY *bustles back down the stairs, in bad humour. He pauses to call back up the stairs.*

PERCY: Give over, woman! I run this pub according to my clientele, not just to suit your Yorkshire puddings! The customer is always right! *(He slams the door and gives a quick embarrassed smile.)* She won't be satisfied until I'm landlord of the public morgue. *(To* VERA.*)* Get your coat off, Vera – we're having afters.

VERA: Percy!

PERCY *(opening the door and yelling up the stairs again)*: You won't! You won't be satisfied until we're sitting tenants in a morgue! I'll tell you something else we're going to have! A piano-smashing competition! That'll bring a bit of life back to the pub! *(He slams the door shut and turns to his customers.)* Who's pally with the landlord of the Stag's Head public house?

COLIN: Charles knows him very well. He did him a favour. He got him that case of Scotch off the back of that lorry.

PERCY *(sourly)*: You never got me no Scotch off the back of a lorry.

CHARLES *(evasively)*: I wasn't doing *him* the favour, Percy – I was doing the favour through him for a different bloke.

PERCY: Well, do me a favour now and get on that telephone.

MICHAEL: It's no use, Percy. We've just been saying – we can't raise a team. There's only Colin comes in here who's big enough to swing a sledge-hammer.

PERCY: There must be somebody else.

COLIN: We're not up to it, Percy, manpower-wise – if God had intended us to enter a piano-smashing competition, he'd have sent us two big regulars, instead of only me.

PERCY: God blimey, we only need *two* men, you say, on sledge-hammers?

MICHAEL: And we've only got the one. So, like Colin says, unless God looks kindly down upon us, and sends

another six foot brawny brainless wonder marching in . . .
good God Almighty!

They follow MICHAEL'*s glance and, with them, we see that
a stranger has entered the pub. He is tall and heavily built.
He is wearing a donkey jacket. His name is* JOHN MULLI-
GAN.

PERCY: Get on that blower to the Stag's Head, Charles.

10 REPRESENTATIVE HONOURS

It is not often that I find myself applauding the statements made by Alan Hardaker, but his pronouncement in a television interview that 'what football wants is more goals', had me bounding out of my chair, on to my feet and waving my rattle. 'Good on yer, Alan,' I cried, and: 'You'll never walk alone!' And when, later in that same television programme, Mr Hardaker went on to point out that men like Matthews and Finney and himself had started their careers in the sport by banging an old tennis ball against a wall, I was waving rhythmically from side to side and chanting, 'Nice one, Alan, nice one, son!'

For I would like to nominate myself as another to be included in that illustrious company named by Mr Hardaker – in fact, I can go even one better than the trio he mentions, for I began my career in football by banging an old tennis ball against *four* walls at the same time. Although, alas, the practice never served to turn me into one of soccer's superstars.

No matter. I tried.

I believe I have mentioned before in these pages that I once played for Scotland in a lavvy-yard? And I am grateful now to Mr Hardaker for giving me the opportunity of examining those internationals of yesteryear in greater detail. For I was turning out regularly for Scotland when I was eight years old, and I played in historic international fixtures against England when goals abounded and we knocked up scores in the region of 35 to 68, or 47 to 53, or even on one insane occasion, 135 to 2. And all of those goal-crazy results were produced with a mangy, balding tennis ball and played out within four short walls.

When we were kids we played our 'footer' in an outside lavvy-yard. These lavvy-yards were evenly spaced out along the terraced streets of back-to-back houses in the north of England, and were built to accommodate the families of four houses each. Every yard contained four water-closets, two dustbins, was about twenty foot square and had towering soot-blackened walls that seemed to soar right up – or so it seemed to us eight-year-olds at least – to *that little tent of blue which prisoners call the sky.* And those selfsame black walls of our own particular lavvy-yard made up the perimeter of our football pitch. It was, looking back, rather like playing in a miniature San Quentin.

We always used to play three-a-side international football in those far-off heady days before the war – or, to be exact, we fielded two boys and one dustbin to each team. Not that we considered the dustbins to be players equal to ourselves in skill or energy, not by any means. No, the fact was that the dustbins were granted their representative honours not because of any outstanding footballing abilities at all but, as fixtures and fittings of the yard, it was easier to include them in the game than it was to lug them out into the street. Besides, even if we *had* taken the trouble to carry them outside, their very presence in the street would have given warning to, and aroused the anger of, their owners who would then have turfed us summarily out of the yard. And so it was that in all International games played at the Lavatory-Yard Ground, Addington Street, Leeds, the England team consisted of two boys and a dustbin, while Scotland was represented by a dustbin and two boys.

On my frail shoulders rested Scotland's hopes. And though it always rankled slightly that I wasn't selected for England, for such was my entitlement by virtue of my birthright – I had some happy days and some exciting and outstanding games with those dustbins.

I played regularly for Scotland because the manager and captain of the Scottish side was a red-haired bull-necked lad named Donald McGuire who threatened to duff me up if I refused the signal honour of joining his squad. Also, it had to be taken into consideration that I stood little chance of making the England team, which consisted of the Kelly brothers, Horace and Jim (and their dustbin), a pair of bandy-legged lads who selected each other and were both big boys for their age. Jim was seven and smoked, Horace was nine and shaved.

The team-sheets then, when we ran out on those long, warm summer evenings, read:

ENGLAND	SCOTLAND
1. Kelly, H.	1. Dustbin, B.
2. Kelly, J.	2. Hall, W.
3. Dustbin, A.	3. McGuire, D.

The sport as practised in that lavvy-yard, dustbins *et al.*, was not as simple or indeed as silly as it sounds. In fact, in restrospect, there was masterly and cunning planning involved in our patterns of play.

Scotland, under the command of its scheming red-headed player-manager, favoured the 1–2 system, i.e.: playing Dustbin, B. in goal and the redoubtable McGuire himself and me up front. By means of this formation, McGuire tacticized, our front runners were thus enabled to pick up any loose balls that flew off Dustbin, B. from mistimed English shots at our goal – in this way we planned to count on quick breakaways, moving from defence into all-out attack with split-second timing.

England, on the other hand, always played a 2–1 formation – having the Kelly brothers in defence, ever-alert for touch-line runs along the lavvy-wall, and utilizing Dustbin A. as a sort of static striker off whom they would hopefully ping deflections and ricochets past our metal keeper.

I have also taken part in trial games where a team has

tried the 1–1–1 system; using the dustbin in midfield, but never with any degree of real success – while a dustbin's distribution might be good, you can never rely on a dustbin as a ball-*winner*.

Well, that's the way we played back in the late 1930s, and I pride myself that much that is good in the sport today has permeated down from those dustbins and the lavvy-yards.

I held my place in that Scottish side for all of one glorious summer before the war – and then suddenly and quite unfairly I was dropped in favour of a bespectacled spotty snotty lad named Royston Pickup. I am not complaining now at being left out, it's a little too late for that. Also, I would be the first to admit that I had a couple of bad games towards the end of my lavvy-yard career: I grew slack at the game and stuck some erroneous and misjudged back-passes to Dustbin, B., our goalie, which slipped past him into our own brickwork netting. But I have always maintained, down the years, that the real

reason I was dropped was because the interloper, Pickup, brought with him a better ball than the ageing tennis one that I had always provided. Pickup's was bigger, albeit multi-coloured (I have always had a sneaking suspicion that he purloined it from a pram).

But they *were* good days, and I would like to see them back again, goal-daft results and all.

So how about it, Mr Hardaker? What do you say to a challenge match? Me and Ted Croker and our dustbin against you and your dustbin and Tom Finney or Sir Stan? And we'll play the game wherever you choose, either at Lancaster Gate or Lytham St Anne's. Better still, how about a neutral ground – say Don Revie's lavvy-yard?

First things first, though.

Does anybody know where I can lay hold of a galvanized iron dustbin? These present-day plastic jobs just haven't got the heart for that good old-fashioned rugged *goal-scoring* football.

11 HANGING THEM UP

Another New Year is upon us and this time I am making a resolution that I fully intend to keep. I am going to hang up my football boots. Believe me, it is not a decision that I have taken lightly. But I am forty-four years old and I feel that my best years in the game are behind me in my scrapbook past.

Not that I have actually *played* football for some years, but I have kept my jock-strap clean and my boots polished – waiting for that elusive phone-call, be it from Alf Ramsey or the secretary of a Sunday morning side. Alas, neither of them bothered to pick up a phone.

And at the start of this new year I am accepting the fact that if I'm not exactly over the top it's only because I haven't got the strength left to climb up there in the first place. The last time I turned out was as buffoon in a Sunday afternoon charity game. After that particular match my skipper, Jimmy Hill, spoke to me in the dressing-room as I gasped and coughed and wheezed.

'If I were you, Willis,' he said, not unkindly, 'I would get out now before I started to slide.'

And if soccer's leading analyst offers you such stout advice, you'd be a fool not to consider it seriously. Besides, I've had my share of the kudos, it's high time I stepped down and gave the younger lads a chance to step into the limelight. Not that it's been roses, roses all the way – I've taken my share of knocks and disappointments, but then that happens to the best of us.

I once got very drunk with a footballer who, in his day, was so famous that to drop his name here would seem a presumptuous liberty. At the time he too was nearing the end of a long career and, naturally, our alcoholic ramblings took a retrospective and maudlin turn.

'Tell me this,' I said to him. 'You have enjoyed a successful and illustrious career, your fame spans many oceans, you have represented our country on more occasions than I have had half-time plastic cups of tea – in short, you have led the life that I and every other man who is a boy at heart would wish to have led, can it be possible that you have any regrets?'

And to my surprise and consternation, the famous footballer fixed me with a sad and sorry eye and blinked. Within seconds, tears were streaming down his face.

'I have never,' he sobbed, 'won an FA Cup-winner's medal.'

And he put his head on my shoulder and wept unashamedly. I allowed him to blub for no more than a moment, and then I lifted him off and spoke to him severely.

'Neither have I,' I said. 'But I'm not crying about it.'

Realizing the sound sense in my remark, he pulled himself together, dried his eyes, and shouted for the barman. There the matter rested and an embarrassing scene had been cleverly averted. Yet I spoke no lie – I never *have* won an FA Cup-Winner's medal – indeed, not even a Loser's gong adorns my mantelpiece.

Taking stock of my playing career, now that it's over, I suppose I must learn to live with the fact that when my call comes to my name writ on the team-sheet of that great Selector-in-the-Sky, I shall report in as a chap who has earned his living by the pen, not by the power in his football boots.

No, schoolboys' idol, I.

On the other hand, I can sit back and appreciate and admire the trophies I have got out of the game, for, without wishing to boast, I think I can honestly claim that I have amassed as good a collection of footballing mementoes and memorabilia as any other fellow – meaning any other fellow like myself who has never kicked a ball in anger or in deadly earnest. Speaking with all due modesty, my collection of soccer trophies may not equal the one on Bobby Moore's sideboard, but on the other hand I feel that I have nothing to be ashamed about.

ITEM: *A bronze medal, 2½ in. in diameter, and inscribed with the legend,* BRUGES STAD.
This is a relic from an ex-internationals' tour of Belgium on which I had scrounged a place as spongeman. During one particular game I enjoyed the signal honour of massaging Billy Wright's knee and also rejoiced in the exalted post of bootboy to Sir Stanley Matthews.

ITEM: *A pair of Leeds United stocking-tabs, number four, that once adorned the calves of Billy Bremner.*
Legend has it that these are the very stocking-tabs worn by the Leeds captain in the 1972 Cup Final, proof of identity being a dark green smudge across the material which, legend claims, was caused by Wembley's lush turf. Legend may be apocryphal. Looking on the black side, the green smudge could have been acquired on the Leeds United training ground when Billy was floored in a practice match by Norman Hunter.

ITEM: *A metal medallion, 1¼ in. in diameter, of simulated gold, bearing the inscription,* WORLD CUP CHAMPION-SHIP. JULES RIMET CUP. ENGLAND. 1966.

And before you start turning up the record books, let me state that I didn't actually *play* for England on that historic occasion – but I was actually *there*, in Wembley Stadium. And the simple medallion I keep as certain proof of the fact, for I bought it in an incoherent drunken stupor at Wembley after our momentous victory – along with vast quantities of T-shirts, tea-towels, key-rings, dish-cloths, lapel-badges, and other souvenirs, all bearing the likeness of one World Cup Willie (Happy Days) – before some good Samaritan poured me into a taxi and pointed it in the vague direction of my home.

ITEM: *An ornate embroidered banner, emblazoned with the flags of two countries and bearing the inscription:* BELGIE–ENGLAND GESPELD TEN VOORDELE VAN UNICEF 5 MEI 1968.

Yet another relic of that Belgian tour, one that was actually handed over on the field of play, before the kick-off, by the captain of their side to the captain of ours. How it comes to be in the possession of the tour's sponge-man and bootboy I am not quite sure – although I sadly suspect it was one more acquisition after a heavy night's drinking, and I would hazard that if the captain of our side reads this piece he will want his banner back.

ITEM: *An impressive silver-plated cup, standing $12\frac{1}{4}$ in., engraved with the legend:* THE TOMMY MERCER TROPHY – FIVE A-SIDE-FOOTBALL – 1968.

To be brutally frank, what this is doing in my home, or how it comes to be in my possession, I have no idea. Was I supposed to present it to someone or did someone, mistakenly, present it to me? Who is Tommy Mercer? Why was someone else, or might it have been himself, perpetuating his name in five-a-side football? Why did they/ he stop? And if they/he haven't/hasn't stopped, what's being used these days for a trophy? If anyone possesses the answers to these and other baffling questions concerning this award, I shall be happy to hear from them. In fact, if the real Tommy Mercer would care to stand up and be counted, he can have his cup back – my wife complains that she has more than her share to polish already.

ITEM: *An ornate medal in simulated silver and gold, $1\frac{1}{2}$ in. in diameter, inscribed:* MORECRAFT CUP – 1967.

We have arrived at the gem of the collection, the Koh-i-Noor of the Willis Hall Soccer Museum, so to speak – for this is an award I got for actually *playing* football. Only for ten minutes or so, admittedly, and that as nonentity substitute for a team of celebrities in a

Sunday afternoon charity game. But I did go on, and we *won*. The meaning of the inscription eludes me – I suspect it is a play on words: MORECRAFT – more craft – get it? The medals were presented by a local bookmaker with a near-Dickensian sense of humour. But let me not decry the award. It is a medal for playing football and winning – and I won it.

And that's the lot. And now that it is written down it doesn't really seem much to show for over thirty years in the game – thirty years of kicks, ploughed fields, cold showers and draughty dressing-rooms. On the other hand, I hope to put the collection to useful purpose.

I have two boys of my own who, as I think I have mentioned before, show no signs of pleasing their father and choosing a career in soccer.

The elder, the six-year-old, has opted for being an attendant in the prehistoric room of the British Museum. The younger, the four-year-old, has expressed a wish that he would like to grow up to be either Emerson Fittipaldi or a horse.

But in the years to come I shall take out my collection of football trophies, polish it, and display it for the benefit of the boys. You never know, it may stir some pride in their young hearts, give them something to aim and strive after.

I tried it out on them last week, without success. They gazed at the separate items dutifully, but somewhat stonily, and then drifted back to their own pursuits – the elder to his prehistoric paintbook, the younger to his sport of knocking over plastic soldiers with Dinky racing cars.

I think I might put my football awards into storage for a couple of years or so. I don't mind. Time is on my side.

12 WORLD CUP 1974

'How would you like,' said Alan Hubbard, the editor, in ominously offhand tones, 'to cover the World Cup for *Sportsworld*?'

'Mmmmm – fine, why not?' I said, trying to sound equally offhanded, while mentally I struggled to remember: when I had last laid eyes on my passport; when I had last had an injection; how many German words had stuck in my memory bank from the BBC's *Colditz* series.

'I mean cover it on the "telly", of course,' said Alan Hubbard.

'Oh, of course,' I replied, lying in my teeth. Although it did occur to me almost immediately that it was probably just as well I wasn't being invited to attend the actual games. I hadn't set eyes on my passport in months, not since the lads had been playing at Foreign Agents at the bottom of the garden. . . . I was so much behind on injections that I would have been baring my upper left arm and gritting my teeth for afternoons on end. The only German words that had remained stuck in my head were *Apfel*, and *Rausraus*, and somebody's name that sounded like 'Major Moan', but probably wasn't spelt like that at all. No, on reflection, I didn't seem somehow ideally equipped to tackle the German football stadii in 1974.

All the same, I was beginning to feel that all too often I was being left holding the wrong end of the stick. Other sportswriters got to go abroad to all kinds of things, and returned sunburnt and all the better for it. I had actually caught them at it.

I am sitting in a hopeless corner of a Heathrow Airport lounge waiting upon delayed holiday transport. I am grasping hold of two kiddies sand-buckets and a toddler-size plastic lavvy seat while snarling at the actual owners of this improbable juvenile equipment. I glance up and observe Hugh McIlvanney, say, strolling across the lounge to board his on-schedule flight with his duty-free Scotch and his romantically battered portable typewriter. Or, Geoffrey Green may cruise through immigration, conversing freely with a couple of international footballers that are to be his travelling companions. I pretend not to notice them and they pretend not to notice me. 'Will you stop bouncing up and down on airport furniture and stop playing with the contents of ash-trays!' I snap, taking it out on the children. I glance around, impatiently, for my wife who sought refuge behind a door marked Femmes *some twenty minutes ago and is still in there, skulking. The toddler-size plastic lavvy seat slips from my nervous fingers and clatters on the plastic flooring. Foreigners in spiky hats turn and look at me and raise their bushy foreign eyebrows.*

The trouble with being primarily a TV playwright is that sports editors tend to think of me as a TV writer primarily. And I am not that at all. Mentally and spiritually, I am a laconic man who sips at a whisky-sour in a jet-liner as he cruises towards Brazil to see Muhammad Ali, or I am a doyen of football writers who chats up Leeds United players in swish bars in swish hotels in far-off places. Why can't other people see me as I see myself?

On occasion, my wife and myself eat out with other sportswriters and their good ladies. Michael and Mary Parkinson have often shared a dining table with us; we have cracked more than one bottle of champagne with Ian and Veronica Wooldridge. And while Mike and I argue in drink the relative merits of Leeds United and Barnsley Football Club; or while I join in academic conversation with Ian Wooldridge, usually in keen and intelligent argument, such as whether or not football is better than cricket – the wives converse about other things. Sportswriters wives are often inclined to make mention of the fact that they see their husbands but seldom.

'He is always off, gadding about on aeroplanes, watching Muhammad Ali in New York or else West Indian cricketers in Jamaica,' someone's wife will murmur.

'Mine isn't,' mutters my missis, darkly. 'He's always under my feet. He just sits at home and mopes and watches television and grumbles when the children want *Doctor Who* on.'

Which isn't altogether true. I go all over the place. I have followed St Albans City Football Club everywhere, as far afield as Woking. I have been known to travel to Luton Town, when Eric Morecambe has been kind enough to invite me. I even went to Wembley in 1974, to watch Bishop's Stortford thrash Ilford in the final of the last Amateur Cup – I was the chap sitting in the right-hand part of the main stand, if you happened to catch the TV snippet.

Well, it is true that I fall a little short on sporting events that have an international interest.

No matter, I was to stay at home throughout June and July, '74, and cover the World Cup for *Sportsworld* sitting in front of my telly. Although, I cannot pretend that even that did not present its problems and I was suffering grim forebodings long before the first kick-off.

'Can't you stop the kids running in and out of the room and firing cap-guns?' I could hear myself saying, and, 'For God's sake, woman, don't you realize that I'm supposed to be watching a quarter-final?'

'You've been watching it for *hours* and there are children's programmes on the other channel.'

'There is football on the other channel,' I imagined myself replying, loftily, 'exactly the same match, in actual point of fact, as the one on this side." One man's Brian Moore is another man's David Coleman.

'Not on BBC2. On BBC2 there's Magic Roundabout.'

'Hang BBC2!' I intended to cry out. 'And hang the Magic Roundabout! How can I sit here watching Mister Zebedee and also lay claim to being *Sportsworld's* TV World Cup Correspondent?'

And, during the above family argument, I was going to miss both the winning goal and the final whistle.

To be absolutely honest, I was really looking forward to it. I am one of the *committed* sportswriters that dearly loves a challenge.

NEW READERS BEGIN HERE: *The editor of* Sportsworld, *jet-setting, fun-loving, Alan Hubbard, has it away to West Germany and the World Cup, leaving mild-mannered sports reporter Willis Hall, to cover the same footballing extravaganza in front of his TV set. Hall, nothing loath, sharpens his pencils and settles back in his armchair.*

NOW READ ON:

I tested my reflexes and toned up my eye muscles for the daunting marathon task of watching TV for the threatened 150 hours by following the England tour games on the telly in the lounge of a small family hotel on the Blackpool seafront while on holiday.

'I wonder if we realize just how lucky we really are in this country?' pondered Jimmy Hill with fervent sententiousness, prior to the screening of the England *v.* Bulgaria match. 'In Bulgaria,' he continued, 'they aren't even screening this game until a few minutes after it has actually started!'

Well, speaking with hindsight now that the World Cup bonanza is over, any country that's willing to forgo the first few minutes of an international football fixture can't be all bad. Neither am I alone in the thought.

When the small family TV set in the hotel lounge cut to the match in progress, four middle-aged ladies of Yorkshire and Lancashire descent collected together their handbags and knitting, got up, and left the room. Their respective husbands settled themselves into more comfortable positions on the not very comfortable small family furniture, relaxed, and prepared to enjoy the game.

It was all, no doubt, a portent of family viewing habits for the madcap weeks to come. And as the games came and went, I stuck it out to the last.

First the ballyhoo preceding the opening of the tournament, then the ballyhoo contained in the opening itself, those sixteen enormous black and white footballs dotted about the Frankfurt pitch and opening out, or so the commentator informed us, 'into colourful petal-shapes'.

The official opening of the 1974 World Cup competition, in fact, was reminiscent of that other European TV junket, *Jeux Sans Frontières* – at least, it had all the camaraderie and colour but seemed a little lacking in its counterpart's frenetic originality. What was needed to whip up excitement, one felt, was Eddie Waring sprinting on to the pitch and telling us that Brazil were playing their joker in the Yugoslavia fixture.

Then, at 3.45 on the afternoon of June 13, 1974, the ballyhoo was over and we were down to the real nitty-gritty. The opposing factions disclosed their true hands, their strengths and their weaknesses, at last.

As usual, despite rumours whipped up by the Press, there were no major shocks. Admittedly, Bill Shankly and Don Revie were missing from the BBC's team-sheet – but news of their non-participation had been leaked days before. And in the ITV camp, Brian Clough had not been named in the side and kicked his heels during the opening game on the substitutes' bench. The teams in the studios at kick-off then, were:

BBC: Hill, J. (Capt.); Mercer, J.; Charlton, B.; McMenemy, L.; McLintock, F.

ITV: Moore, B. (Capt.); Charlton, J.; Crerand, P.; Dougan, D.; Allison, M.

The only mild surprises were ITV's late inclusion of

Ramsey, A. (Sir) as an on-the-spot assistant to Hugh Johns, and the BBC's introduction of the comparatively untried McNenemy, L.

As to turn-out, the BBC took the field in their casual if somewhat staid Beeb regulation strip forgoing jackets and settling for almost formal shirts and neatly knotted ties. While over at London Weekend, the trendies opted for their usual boyish wide ties and even wider lapels. Indeed, Malcolm Allison's haircut was so boyish that it looked as if he'd had it done while sitting on a rocking-horse at Harrods.

And if the opening match on the Frankfurt pitch, between Brazil and Yugoslavia was a dull affair, ending in a draw and with the honours going to Yugoslavia – then the result in the studio could equally be counted a lifeless lack-lustre encounter, but with the edge going to the ITV lads. Both panels, it seemed, frittered away their opportunities, playing tired *bon mots* and flicking excruciatingly bad jokes towards the camera.

'They call 'im Vampire,' twittered BBC panellist Lawrie McMenemy, about a goalkeeper, ''cos he doesn't like crosses!'

But Jimmy Hill seemed hugely amused, and one wondered whether the Beeb had been let down by Basil Brush as well as Shankly and Revie?

The following day we were treated to Chile *v.* West Germany in the late afternoon, and Zaïre *v.* Scotland in the early evening. And in the first match we saw both the first goal of the competition, a worthy one from West Germany's Breitner, and the first sending-off, Chile's Carlos Caszely.

In their respective studios, the BBC opted for different tactics and kept on their jackets, discarding them, though, by the half-time whistle; while ITV, as if to prove to all and sundry that their panel was based on the squad system, dropped Dougan, D., and Charlton, J., bringing in Moncur, R., and the redoubtable Cloughie.

The commercial trendies sneaked an early goal by

turning out in tartan jackets, in Scotland's honour, and won the day by two clear goals having been awarded a penalty for another painful joke committed on the public by Mr McMenemy.

'They call 'im Daffodil,' breezed the Geordie comic, referring this time to a goalkeeper's decision to hug his line, ''cos he only comes out once a year!'

We don't wish to know that – kindly leave the panel! And even J. Hill's engaging smile seemed a little frosty. By Saturday, June 15th, things were really beginning to hot up. Four games to choose from, two on each channel. Nine goals in all from the day's proceedings, and I managed to catch most of them by virtue of my TV control button – more by good luck than judgement, it must be admitted. At the end of that day, we had also been treated to the first good game of the competition: Argentina *v.* Poland, a fixture that had been forecast as a clogging match by the TV pundits.

For these Saturday encounters, the BBC turned out in jackets; over on the other side, the ITV chaps were decked out, to a man, in open-necked sports shirts. A disturbing thought occurred to me: did ITV's football panellists all arrive at the studios similarly dressed because they'd phoned each other up before they'd left home, like the Beverley Sisters?

And what went on in the BBC's studio? Was it an unspoken, mutual decision to appear in shirtsleeve order, or did Jimmy Hill bring his troops into line with last-minute instructions about their battle order?

'Right lads, let's really get stuck into this one – coats off – fixed epigrams and shafts of wit at the ready!' And, if this was the case, was he followed by a last-minute witticism from L. McMenemy? 'They call 'im Potato-Peeler 'ill – 'cos 'e soon 'as us out of our jackets!'

Boom-Boom!

I was an unwilling absentee from some of the second week's matches, being an enforced prisoner in a Manchester Granada TV studio during the early part of the week, where a play of mine (about football, naturally!) was being recorded.

It was, of course, the second week of the World Cup competition when there were matches a-plenty, outsiders went to the wall, and even a few favourites faltered. In the battle for supremacy in viewing figures, too, the first results began to filter in, with something of the hysteria of a General Election.

'We've done it!' was the Beeb's proud boast, with all the bravura of a margarine commercial, 'Three out of every four viewers are watching our coverage!'

The claim seemed, to say the least, to smack of a slight tinge of exaggeration. ITV kept quiet – for ITV's JICTAR ratings are slightly slower out of the starting gates than the Beeb's TAM figures. At a guess, too, I'd say they were rather more accurate.

The ITV figures, when published, claimed that neither company was taking a lion's share of the viewing public who were, in fact, selecting their games on a day-to-day basis, irrespective of particular channel or analytical panel.

Indeed, a fact that was emerging, was that although the actual football was claiming the public's attention, the early evening preview programmes and the late-night match post-mortems were virtually being ignored by the viewers.

Rivalry between the Beeb and ITV had reached such a pitch by this stage of the competition, though, that word came back from Germany that in Frankfurt, where the television troops from both camps were billeted in the same hotel, the BBC had stated in Battalion Orders that its men were not – repeat NOT – to fraternize with the rank and file of the other side under any – repeat ANY – circumstances.

Meanwhile, back in the studios at home, the BBC were beginning to feel that the London Weekend Television lot had stolen a quick march on them by their outright partisanship on Scotland's behalf. For a start, the ITV's

Scottish contingent of two, Paddy Crerand and Bobby Moncur, was double their own representation, Frank McLintock, Coupled with which, the Beeb had never quite recovered from the initial shock it had received when the commercial lads fired their first bullets by turning out in the by-now famous tartan jackets.

The BBC counter-attacked by providing its own panellists with enormous Scottish favours – though tartan rosettes can never be worn with *quite* the same panache as well-cut tartan jackets.

But Scotland, alas, went out of the competition on the evening of Saturday, June 22nd. Dismissed, I fear, not as their eulogists would have us believe, by a bad goal let in by the Zaïre 'keeper against Brazil, but by their own tardiness against the Zaïre side in their opening encounter. On the next day, the Sunday, the only sign of tartan on the TV scene, in the London area at least, was a re-run of the old movie, *Bonnie Prince Charlie*, starring a very un-Scottish David Niven.

For all of us at home, when Scotland went out of the competition a lot of the heart went out of it too – despite the state of euphoria the commentators were enjoying, and enjoining us to enter into, 'Probably the most exciting game of the competition so far,' enthused Brian Moore just before his channel's Holland *v.* Argentine fixture. While at the same time, over on the Beeb, Frank Bough was claiming that the Brazil *v.* East Germany match was 'one the whole world will be watching!'

At half-time, it was Brian Moore who managed a dig at the opposition. 'The Brazil, East Germany game,' he said, barely managing to hide a snigger, 'is by all accounts colourless.'

The second round matches, if nothing else, cleared up a problem that has been puzzling me for years – ever since Sir Alf Ramsey got snooty about his speech and started taking 'electrocution lessons', as Mel Charles once so ingeniously dubbed them. What has always bothered me, is where I've heard that curious 'gee-less' idiom of Sir Alf's before?

'It's surprisin' how close you can come to gettin' a penalty, or how close you can come to not gettin' a penalty,' philosophized the soccer knight, during the Yugoslav *v.* West Germany game, and, 'Helmut Schoen is smilin', the crowd is laughin', shoutin' and cheerin'.' At which point, a curtain lifted in my childhood memory bank. Of course! Eureka! Sir Alf speaks the tongue of Uncle Remus! And henceforth, I shall think of him always not as Sir Alf, but *Brer* Alf.

The second round matches came and went – remarkable only for the ungallant exit made by Brazil; the end of a once-proud legend. The latter games took place, we were all surprised to discover, with almost startling infrequency. Even the non-sports-loving viewers who had complained at the start of the competition at how much football they were being threatened with, were surprised in the closing stages at what little they actually got.

Still, they had other things to complain about: the whole of Wimbledon; the England *v.* India Third Test; the 103rd Open golf championship looming over the horizon. . . . There was so much sport on our own doorstep, that some of us almost forgot that the World Cup was still going on in somebody else's backyard.

Final honours went, at last, to the host nation. If nothing else, that gave most of us a chance to say 'I *told* you so!' – for though nearly all of us had changed our minds at some point in the competition, hadn't we each and everyone tipped West Germany before the shindig started?

As for the studio tussle, I T V held their two goal lead, thus proving the inestimable value of the squad system. And if it wasn't the most exciting of World Cup competitions, at least the panellists seemed to enjoy it. Perhaps, in four years' time in Argentine we'll have something to *really* get het up about. . . .

All together now, with me in keen anticipation, clap hands, Viva Don Revie and 'England, England. . . .'

13 EVACUATION OF AN ENGLAND CAPTAIN

To the five-year-old it was an alien word which belonged to the strange and mysterious world of the adult vocabulary: Evacuation. It was one of those words that he had already learned to be wary of, words that ended with 'shun', like immunization and conscription and mobilization and invasion. War-time words. He was aware vaguely, that there was something called a war on.

Evacuation was one of those words which caught his parents on the hop if he ran into a room unexpectedly and heard them using it. They would start chattering away forty to the dozen about something else but, all the time, shooting him those odd parental glances, and he knew instinctively that they had just been discussing something to do with his own immediate future. And, in a child's world, for a long, long time, evacuation was just another word.

Then, as the phoney war dragged on, the word began to take on a real meaning. Evacuees – they were just kids, like himself. He saw them every Saturday afternoon on the Paramount News at the two-penny rush. 'The Eyes And Ears of The World'. Great gangs of kids standing around on railway stations, clutching attaché cases and bulging pillow-slips, cardboard gasmask cases slung round their necks, indelibly marked luggage labels dangling from their lapels. They clambered into railway carriages lugging their belongings like a miniature British Expeditionary Force, some of them even aping the manners of the real one. They stuck their thumbs in the air and grinned cheekily for the benefit of the news-cameramen, at least some of them did – some of the smaller ones were crying.

And then it wasn't long before it was the turn of the kids from his own school who were going and, in a way, he envied them and their new homes and their new freedom. He went down to the schoolyard one wet Saturday morning to see them off. They seemed an aggressively unhappy little group and none of them stuck their thumbs in the air, they just moped in the playground waiting for the bus to come while the teachers fussed round them, unusually considerate, wiping their noses and forming them into groups. He said a few goodbyes through the school railings in the adult way in which children say goodbye.

'See yer, Haynesy.'

'Yer. See yer Chuck.'

'Yer.'

But he didn't hang around very long and the man from the Paramount News with the magical camera never showed up. Besides, he had to run home for an early lunch so as to be in time for the local flea-pit that afternoon; Flash Gordon was to do battle with the Clay Men, adversaries who were far more threatening to a schoolboy than the looming menace of the Luftwaffe.

The country was still playing at war and its children were only playing at evacuation then. Whole train-loads of kids would set off for that distant, promised land: The Country – and within a week a dribble of dissatisfied and homesick wanderers would begin to filter back.

'Hiya, Haynesy!'

'Hiya, Chuck! What was it like then?'

'Rotten. How did Flash Gordon get on?'

The war was soon forgotten and the Blitz was yet to come.

There was, still, the occasional empty desk in the classroom. There were those enviable children, members of a vaunted and élite society, who had been evacuated so far afield that it was not possible or conceivable that they should come back. The ones who had journeyed to Southampton and gone down to the sea in ships – to Canada and to the United States of America, where the film stars came from. They were the special ones. And when he saw *them* on the Paramount News he knew they were special, because they had Gracie Fields or Vera Lynn to see them off on the boatdeck, wishing them luck as they waved them goodbye. Sometimes he even heard them on the wireless, sandwiched in between perpetual news broadcasts, lisping quavering messages across oceans to their mums and dads. On such occasions, his own parents went back into that peculiar adult vocabulary he had grown to recognize and mistrust, and whispered words like torpedoes and magnetic mines, and looked at him and shook their heads, emphatically.

It was 1940, the bombing had started, and he was six years old, when evacuation uprooted him for the first time from Edmonton and Houndsfield Road Council School, and set him down in the heart of the country. But his first exile from London and his schoolmates was to be short-lived.

At the time, he wasn't even aware of the fact that he was being evacuated; looking back now he has little clear memory of that first excursion into country living. He has been told since that it was his father's decision that his mother and himself should be deposited in the safety of the country for the duration. And he does, distantly, remember the morning when his father took them both to the station, put them on a train, and that they eventually arrived at a small village on the outskirts of Braintree, Essex. Of where they stayed, and of whom they stayed with, he remembers nothing – and the only thing that he is clear about is that they didn't stay there very long – four days to be exact. His mother didn't take too kindly to the disjointing of the family and, when she saw a fruit and vegetable lorry clearly marked with its point of destination, Enfield, trundling along a country lane towards them, the temptation was too great. Enfield is, after all, no more than a turnip's throw from Edmonton. Mrs Haynes seized Johnny by the hand, flagged down the lorry and, pausing only long enough to pick up their belongings, they were both perched up in the driver's cab and heading back towards home.

Mr Haynes received them back into the home without surprise or comment and, for the time being at least, the subject of evacuation was forgotten. The following day young Haynes was back at Houndsfield Road without arousing much excitement.

'Hiya, Chuck!'

'Hiya, Haynesy! What was it like then?'

'Rotten. How did Flash Gordon get on?'

The dialogue was familiar.

But Flash Gordon was soon to take up an increasingly smaller part of his life; the inter-planetary wanderings of that war-time astronaut began to play second fiddle to a new-found interest – it was about that time that the boy began to take football seriously. A number of the star players of the Houndsfield Road School football team had been transferred by virtue of evacuation, and at the age of seven Haynes was turning out pretty regularly for the school Juniors.

Oddly enough, it was the war, or rather its attendant shortages which caused him to take a greater interest in the game than he otherwise might have done. His mother's local Edmonton greengrocer, a rabid football fan, was taking a great interest in the fading fortunes of the Houndsfield Road School Football Team. It seems, now, an odd sort of club to gain the interest of a grown man. But in those days soccer matches of any kind weren't all that easy to come by; the football addict of the early forties had to course his adrenalin where he could.

Now, the greengrocer was not a man overburdened with scruples when it came to seeing his champions on the winning end, and he offered the boy – an amateur schoolboy player – an illegal bonus incentive: an orange for every three balls he put into the back of the net. An orange for every three goals would not be considered, by present-day standards, sufficient to make the average Junior player raise an eyebrow. Even to this day, Haynes is not quite sure whether the greengrocer was a hard and demanding taskmaster, or whether oranges were really all that hard to come by. But, at the time, and offered to a growing schoolboy, the incentive was more than enough. Haynes didn't pause to argue terms with his self-appointed manager – he settled down at Houndsfield Road to tuck home goals and by so doing earn oranges as fast as he could.

There was still a war on and, as he grew older, he was becoming progressively aware that, somewhere, it was all happening. Indeed, that issues of war-time living were encroaching on the day-to-day life at Houndsfield Road School. The bigger lads were collecting scrap-metal in home-made barrows; some of the luckier ones were even enjoying whole nights of adventurous freedom on a mysterious excursion called fire-watching; others toured the classrooms with ever-present collecting boxes labelled Red Cross or Spitfire Week. There were also those who expended their surplus energy Digging For Victory on the school allotments. Happily, the school allotments never extended on to the playing fields and, for one carefree seven-year-old, the football season of 1941/42 passed pleasurably – and he was getting more than his fair share of Vitamin C. By the time the following football season came round he was a year older, and he looked forward with eager anticipation to the extra oranges that would be within his compass now that he had put on an inch or so in height.

At the age of eight he was football crazy and nothing else mattered. It was then that the blow fell.

'See yer, Haynesy.'

'Yer. See yer, Chuck.'

'Yer.'

For, in October of that year, his parents took the decision to evacuate him for a second time. He pleaded.

He protested. He spent hour after vain hour pointing out the inevitable consequences of such a rash act – not only what it would mean to the school football team, but the heart-ache and pain that would be suffered by the local greengrocer. He could have saved his breath. The weight of his argument was useless.

He supposes, looking back, that his final excursion into the country could not be classified as an official evacuation. It was certainly not organized under the auspices of the London County Council. There was no gathering in the playground to wave goodbye; no luggage label hanging round his neck, no cluster of teachers to pamper his departure; no cups of WVS tea on the station platform. There was certainly no Paramount News cameraman to record his leavetaking for the benefit of local cinema audiences. He was one small boy put on one large train, and in his heart there was a void as big as Wembley Stadium.

The industrial north presents, at the best of times, an unwelcoming picture to the visitor. Undeniably, there is a warmth to be found beneath the grim exterior, but to the new arrival it has little to offer as far as the eye is concerned. The belching tall chimneys, the grime-blackened factories, the endless chains of row upon row of back-to-back terrace houses – even the public parks in the north are overburdened with dour, mirthless, aldermanic statues where there ought to be goalposts.

As the train carried him farther and farther into the heart of the cotton-mill belt, he pressed his nose to the window and gazed at a passing show in comparison with which Edmonton seemed like gracious rural living.

He shared a compartment, he remembers, with a couple of soldiers who were off on a few days' snatched leave. They were friendly enough, but their unfamiliar hard vowels had, to the boy, the ring of a foreign language. Indeed, as far as the lad was concerned, the north of England *was* a foreign country. He had, in his young life, encountered travelled relatives who had journeyed on pre-war trips to Boulogne – but nobody within his experience had travelled as far afield as – where was it? – Droylesden, Lancs.

The couple who were to take him into their home met him at the station, and a short bus-ride later he was in his new home and alone in his new bedroom. They had only one child, a boy of about the same age as himself, and it was with him that he was to share the bedroom. However, the other lad was at school when he arrived, which gave him the chance to make a close examination of his new surroundings by himself. He sat perched on the end of his bed and had a good look round. He wandered about the room, opening every drawer and cupboard and examining the possessions of his absent room-mate: his shirts, his ties, his socks – until he tired of the pastime. The stranger's wardrobe seemed, on average, pretty much on a par with his own and led him to the comforting conclusion that there couldn't be all that much difference between himself and the strange breed of humanity into which he had been flung in the alien land. He even examined, with great curiosity, the newspaper linings at the bottom of the drawers, printed in the unfamiliar type of unfamiliar northern newspapers. Then, having cased the room to his own satisfaction, he crossed to the window and gazed out at the strange sky-line – staring hard and long and trying to will it into familiarity.

Later – much later – he went downstairs and handed over his official credentials, his ration book and clothing coupons. He was part of another family.

This second term of exile was, if duration is to be taken as a yardstick, more successful than the first; he languished on the outskirts of Manchester for four months. Looking back, it seems now that the suburbs of that great industrial city were an unlikely place to look for shelter from Hitler's long-range bombers but, at the time, it was London that was taking the plastering and the north of England was considered comparatively safe.

The family he stayed with was kind, considerate, and

went out of its way to make his stay a pleasant one – but a child has only one home, and he had always been very attached to his. Not that he was ever desperately homesick; there never seemed time for that, and the friendship of the son of the house went a great deal of the way towards making up for the rift from his own family. But he was never really happy at his new school. Children, it's said, make friends easily. This may be true, but they are also cautious in new alliances. And nothing ever supplants the security of the friendship that exists between kids who have grown up together. And although he made many friends in Manchester, they were all of them surface friendships – the local school-children never *quite* trusted his Cockney accent, nor, for that matter, did he ever come to terms with their northern speech idioms. And, although he made friends, he never made the grade in northern schools' league football – much to his disgust. Perhaps it was his own fault. Perhaps he never really fancied that peculiar brand of the game they played on those aptly-named 'cinder-pitches'. Perhaps he was fretting for those bonus oranges that were not to come. Perhaps, even in those far-off days, he was a one-club man – for he is ready to admit now that he never truly played his heart out in the north in the way that he had at Houndsfield Road.

Four months passed. It seemed, then, an interminable sentence but it *was* only four months.

His mother it was who decided that, Hitler or no Hitler, home was where young Johnny Haynes belonged, and the lad himself was happy to agree. He cannot now look back and claim that those restless years had even the slightest effect on his future life. He remembers that when he returned to Houndsfield Road school after his last four-month enforced absence he was greeted as if he had not been gone.

'Hiya, Chuck!'

'Hiya, Hayensy! What was it like then?'

'Rotten. How's the team been getting on?'

'Rotten.'

And school life went on.

The following Saturday, his name was one of that happy, elected band on the school notice-board chosen to play that same afternoon. For one eight-year-old the war might not have been on. Evacuation was, after all, just a word once again.

He pulled on his school-colours, tied up his stockings, and ran out on to the Houndsfield Road football pitch. It was one of the happiest days in the life of Johnny Haynes. He scored eight times that afternoon. The local green-grocer, in his exultation, presented Haynes with three congratulatory oranges.

14 WHISTLE, AND I'LL COME TO YOU

On one particular Sunday morning, while most of the country's soccer buffs lay abed, hugging the blankets and sulking to themselves over England's drubbing the previous day at the hands of Bremner & Co. at Hampden Park, I was up at the crack of dawn – well, almost – and met with some hundred or so battle-scarred campaigners of the field who were joined together to scheme, plan and counter-plan their tactics for the bitter struggles that they knew were yet to come.

No, I wasn't out on manoeuvres with week-end guerrillas or illegal revolutionaries, quite the reverse, in point of fact. For the gentlemen in question were *up-holders* of the law, football referees of all grades who had got together on a refresher course and conference.

A happy band of those gallant and eager hearties who view the world with their own particular vision, a world in which: a coin is something to be tossed before a game; a handkerchief is an article with which to wipe mud from a goalkeeper's eye; a notebook and pencil a means of recrimination; a pocket-watch a piece of equipment designed solely to measure forty-five minutes of play.

The annual conference of the Hertfordshire Referees Association was taking place in Welwyn Garden City, and this year the emphasis was to be on 'the younger, junior, or greener referee, officiating on the local parks'. Which seemed to be a good idea. Hertfordshire is rife with park and Sunday football. And Sunday football, as every match official worth his whistle knows, is the ideal sport for embryo referees to sharpen their teeth and pencils on. Sunday morning footballers are inclined to enjoy more early showers than they are hot Sunday dinners. And Hertfordshire suffers from Sunday football in the way that some places suffer a rash of measles – except, alas, that Sunday football is a good deal harder to cure.

Welwyn Garden City, at half-past nine of a Sunday morning, could hardly claim to be bursting with life, and I homed in easily on the conference hall by the sound of referees' intimidating laughter over pre-refresher-course coffee. Incidentally, what *is* the collective noun for a number of match officials? A 'caution' of referees? An 'offside' of linesmen? No matter, there was this collection of mob-handed referees, sipping their coffee, chatting together and hailing old acquaintances they had not set eyes on, one imagined, since they had shared baths and games together in seasons gone by.

Looking back, I'm not sure what I had expected a hundred referees *en masse* would look like – it transpired that they looked like ordinary folk. Put a hundred foot-ballers together in one place and they would look like footballers – but a hundred referees in everyday clothes would win a ton of certificates from the *What's My Line* panel on any Saturday afternoon. For the record though and also for the benefit of fans who are wont to scream out 'Where's your glasses, ref?' from the terraces, there was not a pair of spectacles in sight.

It was to the assemblage's credit that it had got together during term-time, for surely many of them must still have been regaining their breath from the previous day's exertions? I cannot speak for the rest of the country, but minor football in the county of Hertford-shire continues long after the season ends. While the big boys in the Football League have got the good sense to put their boots away at the proper time, the amateurs who turn out ostensibly for the love of the game, go on huffing and puffing, hoofing at the ball and each other, in places where by natural sporting right, there should be wickets laid.

The referees' conference was in the capable hands of a Mr Syd Stoakes, himself an ex-referee and now a leading instructor for the FA. Mr Stoakes not only knows his football, he also knows how to tell it. Speaking for myself, if I had had my fill of football last season, I had been totally *gorged* of football verbiage from TV's analysts and commentators. The only man that I can listen to for any length of time on football is Ron Greenwood who, for my money, is informative, intelligent and entertaining – while these days most of television's soccer talk seems uninformed, unintelligent and *dull*. I would like it to be known that the FA's Syd Stoakes is entitled to sit on Ron Greenwood's right hand whenever he likes.

After Mr Stoakes had given his introductory lecture, the referees split up into separate discussion groups to debate the sort of subjects that referees are inclined to debate: 'Postponement, Suspension & Abandonment,' 'Discipline', Control Techniques' and 'Briefing Linesmen'.

I weighed in with the 'Discipline' bunch and events

quickly assured me that I had made a wise choice. As a man of the theatre, I thoroughly enjoyed watching referees go out to the front of the class and improvise little cameos as to their methods of cautioning dissident players, or even sending them off.

'I *saw* that,' growled out one referee-cum-thespian, waving an obligatory admonishing finger. 'That was an unnecessary foul and I am cautioning you for dangerous play. Can I have your name?' And, delighted with his own performance, the referee turned to the rest of his class for approbation. He had his critics, though.

'You can't caution a player for dangerous play,' said a fellow match-official. 'The FA won't accept it.'

'The FA won't,' another worthy was quick to point out, 'but the *Herts* FA will.'

For a moment it seemed as if pedanticism was about to run rife.

A referee rose to his feet and told a sad and sorry tale of how he had once cautioned a player, 'Wilkins, M.', and that it later transpired that the team contained two 'Wilkins, M.', Michael and Maurice, a pair of brothers. A murmur of refereeing sympathy ran round the room, and it was the considered opinion of the discussion group that first name initials were insufficient where bookings were concerned.

It was all enthralling stuff.

At eleven-twenty, the referees trooped back into the main hall to summarize their findings and invite the comments of the admirable Mr Stoakes. They were still arguing the toss, in the nicest possible way, when I stole out of the hall shortly after twelve o'clock. And they were to continue with similar lecture and debate, on subjects as diverse as: 'Recognition of Intent' and 'Fouls and Misconduct' and 'Goalkeepers, Offences By and Against', throughout the afternoon, with intervals signalled for lunch and tea, of course.

As I drove home through the green heart of the Hertfordshire countryside, I could hear the occasional cry of

Sunday footballers coming up from Sunday football playing fields.

'Do me a favour, ref!'

'Didn't you *see* that, ref, have you gone *blind*?'

'Did you hear what he called you, ref, are you going to let him get away with it?'

'Referee, why don't you get off the bloody pitch?'

But when the shouts had died away, I paused to consider that on that particular Sunday morning an approximate hundred match officials, from every level of the game, who receive scant payment and less thanks for their labours, had each paid one pound fifty and given up a whole day in order to discuss not what they could get out of football, but what they might put into the game.

There are moments, rare but rewarding, when I'm almost optimistic about the future of the sport.

15 BOARD MEETING

From *A Song at Twilight*, BBC TV 1973

The scene is the boardroom of a Football League club. Seated around the boardroom table are three of the club's directors: PERCY BOLTON, EDWARD STIGGINS *and* JOSEPH GATLEY. BILLY MEADOWS, *the club chairman, is at the head of the table.* AUSTIN MELCROFT, *the club secretary, bustles in with an armful of agenda and other documentation, and the meeting gets under way:*

MELCROFT: 'Apologies for lateness, Mr Chairman – everyone.'

MEADOWS *(brusque and businesslike)*: I'm sure you had an excellent reason, Austin, shall we press on? Agenda?

MELCROFT *hands out the typewritten agendas, as* MEADOWS *continues:*

MEADOWS: And shall we take last week's minutes as read – in the interests of expediency?

MEADOWS *looks round at his directors inquiringly, at the same time stabbing a finger at* STIGGINS *and another at* GATLEY. *The two men raise their hands, signifying that they propose and second the previous week's minutes.*

MEADOWS: Proposed-and-seconded-last-week's-minutes -as-read.'

During the above, MELCROFT *has handed out the agenda and has sat down with the minutes book. He is now riffling through his documentation, officiously, as* MEADOWS *continues:*

Draw your attentions to Items One. Items One: Public Urinals at the Garrison Road End . . .

MELCROFT *(having located two letters)*: Before we continue, Mr Chairman, bring to your notice, apology for absence from last week's meeting, Mr Copthorne, his good lady, Mrs Copthorne, has written in – he's been whipped into hospital, not at all well.

MEADOWS: Apology accepted. Items One . . .

MELCROFT: Before we continue with Item One, Mr Chairman, if I might crave the attention of the meeting once again?

MEADOWS *(grudgingly)*: Feel free, Mr Secretary.

MELCROFT: Apologies for absence from tonight's meeting, Mr Copthorne, his good lady, written in again no improvement, he's – er – still in dock.

MEADOWS: Apologies accepted. You might drop her a note, Austin, sympathizing. And on to Items One: Public Urinals, Garrison End . . . (BOLTON*'s hand has crept up in the air.)* Yes Percy?

BOLTON: If I might, er . . .? Regarding Frank Copthorne's unfortunate illness, I have been keeping a weather-eye open, as per pro – it would seem that there are grave doubts as to whether or not our worthy co-director will last the week out. His ticker – heart. I just wonder if we should consider the actions of the board in the case of an untimely sad event?

MEADOWS *(testily)*: Items One, on my agenda, reads Public Urinals, Garrison Road End. There's no reference here to untimely sad events. I'd say, untimely sad events came under the general umbrella of Any Other Business items eight. Shall we carry on for now with Public Urinals, Garrison Road End, Item One? *(*MELCROFT *is wiggling his Biro in the air.)* Yes, Austin?

MELCROFT: Mr Chairman, bring to your attention, Item Seven.

MEADOWS: Item Seven, Manager's Report. What about it, yes?

MELCROFT: We've had a request to upgrade Item Seven, Manager's Report to Item One on the agenda, Mr Chairman.

MEADOWS: Mr Secretary, Item Seven, Manager's Report, as you are surely well aware, is specifically itemized at Item Seven in so far as any items arising out of Items Seven, Manager's Report, can be fully discussed under Any other Business, Item Eight.

MELCROFT: Point fully taken, Mr Chairman. Only the club manager, Mr Ritchie, requested me to request you as to whether it might be possible to bring forward Item Seven, Manager's Report, to Item One – only if possible, of course – as he has recourse to attend a game tonight over at the City ground, in order to watch a player he's interested in.

MEADOWS *sighs, heavily, and catches sight of* GATLEY *trying to catch his eye.*

MEADOWS: Yes, Joseph?

GATLEY: Just a suggestion, but might it not be possible to upgrade Item Seven, Manager's Report, to Item One, and also as it were upgrade Item Eight, Any Other Business, to Item Two, thus downgrading Item One, Public Urinals Garrison Road End, to Item Three? Ensuring that any Items arising out of Item Seven – as you were – Item *One*, Manager's Report, could be discussed and gone into as and when they arise, following upon the relevant item – if you see what I mean?

MEADOWS: We can hardly upgrade Any Other Business to such a unique position on the agenda. I mean, that's just making a mockery of the entire agenda procedure as laid down since time immemorial, *quid pro quo!*

STIGGINS: Hear, hear!

MEADOWS: Items Seven, Manager's Report, upgraded to Item One. All right, Austin, wheel him in.

MELCROFT *rises, crosses and opens the door.* EDDIE RITCHIE, *the manager, enters.* RITCHIE *is an ex-player in his early fifties. A battle-scarred campaigner who spent his playing career filling the left-back position for a host of Third and Fourth Division clubs. He marches across to the board-room table and comes to a halt, awkwardly.*

94

RITCHIE: Mr Chairman, gentlemen.

He gets a cold glance from the Chairman and quick embarrassed smiles from the directors.

RITCHIE: Beg to present my report for the month ending April 29.

He pauses. MEADOWS *nods for him to continue.* RITCHIE *clears his throat and stands at ease. He takes a couple of grubby, wrinkled sheets of notepaper from his inside pocket and smooths them out. He lays them down on the table and leans over them, placing his knuckles on the table in order to read the notes. He studies the notes for some moments, in silence, his lips moving soundlessly then, realizing that the pages are in the wrong order, swoops them round.* MEADOWS, *eyebrows raised, gives his directors a long-suffering glance.* RITCHIE *glances up.*

RITCHIE: I shan't bore you with facts and figures and I won't beat about the bush. (*Another glance at his notes, then*): We've had our good games and our bad games, but it's results that count and, in the final analysis, if you aren't getting the results you're not doing your club or yourself any good. That's my candid opinion. (*Another glance at his notes.*) We haven't been getting the results. (*He pauses to examine both his pages of notes carefully, then decides to dispense with them entirely.*) No matter how you look at it – examine it how you will – lost four, drawn one does not smack of true success. On the other hand, looking for a little light in the darkness, the draw *was* away from home, a ruddy hard match, and a good one to nick a point from. And two of the four we went down on were no disgrace: we played hard, we deserved to win, they ran their ruddy legs off on the park for me, they fought for every ball those lads. . . . All right, face facts, we were beat by better teams. But you don't want me to come in here, month after month, and make excuses. I'm the one that carries the can, in the final analysis. In the final analysis, I don't get paid to stand here and say that we got tonked by better teams than us. Because you know, and I know, that in the final analysis, I get paid my wages to see to it that there *are* no better teams than us. I wish to God I could say I had done my job. It's my personal ambition to have the best club side in Europe out there on that park – bar none! *(A pause, he smiles wistfully, lost in a private fantasy, then)*: Coming back to earth again, what's to be done? Putting the past behind us – Correction, I know that we *can't* put the past behind us, what's done is there in the record books. But now we have to build towards *next* season. It's like – you know – kiddies' building bricks. Somebody knocks them over so you have to start again, building them up, from scratch.

MEADOWS *(dangerously calm)*: In a lower division, do you mean?

RITCHIE: If we wish to face facts – yes.

MEADOWS: Don't you mean, if we wish to admit defeat?

RITCHIE: No. I mean what I say, face facts. It's not a question of winning any longer, is it? It's a question of hoping other clubs are going to lose, do us a favour, drop points.

GATLEY: Isn't it a question of who's to blame for that situation cropping up?

STIGGINS: Hear, hear!

RITCHIE: Do you mean, who's going to carry the can?

MEADOWS: Gentlemen, gentlemen! We do not brook talk of can-carrying at this club. We stand behind the staff that we appoint, we've always been noted for that. I'm sure we *all* appreciate *and* admire *and* applaud the efforts that our manager has made on behalf of the club – over and above a manager's norm.

STIGGINS: Hear, hear!

RITCHIE: I'm a club man.

MEADOWS: I think I speak for all concerned when I say that fact is recognized and highly esteemed.

There are half-hearted grunts of approval from the directors.

RITCHIE: Many thanks. In return, just like to say, appreciate your confidence. *(He pauses, embarrassed at his own emotion, and clears his throat before he continues.)* It's a question *really* isn't it, of what steps we propose to take appertaining to our future interests. The – er – reason I asked to address you early on this evening is because I'd like to see a bit more strength up front. Consequently, I'm going over to the game at the City ground tonight in order to have a look at a lad.

MEADOWS: We *need* somebody up front. Might we enquire . . . er . . .?

RITCHIE: This lad Forshaw, I've been hearing some very good reports.

BOLTON: He's superb. . . .

STIGGINS: Unquestionably . . .

BOLTON: I've had recourse to watch him on the box.

GATLEY: He wins balls, he not only scores, he *wins* the ball as well.

MEADOWS: Only, the whole point is, Eddie, there's a little bird been flying round with a rumour that the City's asking seventy thousand for him.

RITCHIE: I had heard.

MEADOWS: We haven't *got* seventy thousand.

STIGGINS: Not at this immediate moment.

MEADOWS: Not to spare.

GATLY: Cash in hand.

(An awkward pause.)

RITCHIE: No. Well. No harm in having a look at the lad. If only for future reference.

MEADOWS: No harm at all. Six-forty-five. You should be on your way.

RITCHIE: Yes – right.

RITCHIE *nods at them all in turn, taking his leave.*

MEADOWS: Before you go – I would like it to go on official record, on behalf of my fellow-directors and the club, that we are all cognizant of the difficulties you are labouring under: injuries, bad luck, not getting the run of the ball. We would just like it to be understood – like you to know – that we are behind you in this board room one hundred and one per cent.

STIGGINS: And so say all of us.

MEADOWS: Every inch of the way that is.

RITCHIE *(touched)*: Thank you, most sincerely, one and all. Good night. God bless.

MEADOWS: Enjoy the game!

RITCHIE *goes out and* MELCROFT *closes the door on him.*

MEADOWS: It's not a bit of use – we'll have to get shot of him.

MELCROFT *(Biro poised)*: Any Other Business, shall I put it down as?

MEADOWS: Yes, Austin. Items Eight, Any Other Business, subpara 'A', Managerial Seat, Forthcoming Vacancy Of. *(Briskly.)* And if I might refer you back to your agenda, gentlemen, pushing on, we do have a long evening ahead – Items Two, Public Urinals, Garrison Road End. Who's going to push the boat out?

They refer to their agenda.

16 DEAR MR REVIE

From *Sportsworld*, 1973

Or may I call you Don? I sincerely hope so, considering the close association and success we've enjoyed together over the years. In case you haven't tumbled to me yet, I'm the chap who manages the team. The *other* chap. Admittedly, you do your share at the training ground, and what happens every Saturday afternoon I'll willingly give you credit for. But come on, Mr Revie, sir, come clean – I haven't been doing too badly for the lads myself, results-wise. And I was at Elland Road before you took the chair.

The first time I took a hand in the club's destiny was so long ago now that I don't care to remember the year; suffice it to say that another chap called Major Buckley held the reins and we were struggling more than half-way down the Second Division.

I was struggling myself at the time – with the script of a radio play I was working on for the Midland and North Regional Service of the BBC. I cannot, looking back, remember the plot of that piece, only that it required that at some point the football results be read out. With barely a moment's hesitation, I slipped into the script the heartening score: Barnsley 0, Leeds United 3 – and as far as listeners in the Midland and North Region were concerned, Leeds had gained their first away victory in weeks (albeit a fictional one).

On the face of it, looking back, I suppose it might seem a small achievement, one hardly worthy of recall. Certainly the play was no great shakes as a piece of drama. But for one brief moment during the transmission of that play, a small percentage of Leeds United supporters (for I'm ready to admit that the percentage of Leeds fans who listen to broadcast dramatic works is probably minuscule), had heard a pleasing result and were themselves cheered. Eureka! The fading fortunes of the club had taken a happy turn, if only in the land of story-tale and make-believe.

That was how it all began. Tall oaks from little acorns grow.

Since that date, those many long years ago, and under my inspired fictional managership, Leeds United FC has not looked back – the team has triumphed through many hard and bitter battles fought out in acted dramas both on sound radio and on television. I am able to boast, throughout the years, guided by me, they have not lost a game and neither have they dropped one single point.

Mr Revie – sir – you will understand, forgive, and even possibly share my pride.

In the mid-fifties, I steered us through to victory at Wembley in the FA Cup by the mere insertion of a couple of lines of dialogue heard over a trawler's crackling radio receiver during a television dramatized documentary concerning the herring fleet.

In the early sixties, a thriller I wrote for 'the box' incorporated the first Cup and League double for the club – a triumph, I might add, that we have since repeated on a couple of occasions, both astutely managed and both richly deserved.

The *Budgie* television series was total grist to the mill of United. Or almost. *Budgie* was scripted by myself and Keith Waterhouse. And though Mr Waterhouse's writing is never less than admirable, he would be the first to admit that his soccer knowledge leaves much to be desired. Had it not been for my swift intervention in Episode Thirteen, Waterhouse would have had the lads going down to Darlington at home! Think nothing of it, Mr Revie, sir, I only did what any right-minded scriptwriter would have done.

During the twenty-four episodes of the series, Budgie

himself, an avid football fan, trudged away from every London football ground having seen the home side lose to my Elland Road invincibles. We even had the gall to take two points at Stamford Bridge when Charlie Endell, Budgie's villainous employer, was sitting in the directors' box.

Aficionados of the *Budgie* series will recall that Budgie's mum was unlucky enough to pass away while Leeds United were trouncing Spurs at White Hart Lane (an early goal from Bremner and a second nodded home before half-time by Clarke). Budgie was absent on that occasion but his father, a Spurs supporter, suffered the first half until the ground's loudspeaker system summoned him to his good lady's deathbed. What a way to go.

A Thirty Minute Theatre play for BBC TV entitled *They Don't All Open Men's Boutiques* was about a team that was due to face Leeds United in the FA Cup, and the viewer was left in little doubt as to who the eventual winners would be. And, if doubt there was, I cleared that up in a BBC Play for Today, in which Leeds United coasted home comfortably by *five* goals to nil.

No, but seriously, Mr Revie – sir – I know the lads are doing all right for you, but they aren't knocking home *quite* as many goals for you as they do for me. Over the years, I think my record speaks for itself:

PLAYED	LOST	DRAWN	WON	GOALS FOR	GOALS AGAINST
12	0	0	12	57	0

What can't speak can't lie.

Mark you, Mr Revie – sir – I have no wish to grab all of the credit for myself. A lot of the hard graft, both on and off the field *is* down to you. And I've played the side, as often as not, in the numbered shirts as you have called them – though I prefer to think of this more as a question of great minds thinking alike. I have never, for example, considered such an example as Sir Alf contrived when he played Norman Hunter in midfield. No, what has been achieved, Mr Revie, I like to think of as being achieved by both of us together – it's just that my own contribution seems to have gone by largely unnoticed. . . . .

What I'm getting at is – I've scratched your back long enough, isn't it time that mine got just a tickle in exchange from you? Now – there's the new play I'm struggling with for London Weekend Television, deadline for delivery is Tuesday week . . . Mr Revie – sir – or may I call you Don? – how are you at play construction or do you have an ear at all for dramatic dialogue?

17 THE GOOD BOARDROOM GUIDE

Having spent what seems like a lifetime in watching football – indeed, the hapless performances of my own team this season have oftimes made it seem more like a life-*sentence* – I have finally come full circle in my role of spectator.

I have opted to stand out on the terraces where I began my career as a fan.

Over the years, I have stood or sat out the game from almost every conceivable vantage point: a seat in the stand; a season ticket for a tip-up seat; a position in the press-box; an invitation from high places into the directors' box; I have even spent a couple of seasons sitting on the trainer's bench – you name it, I've tried it. And after all my wide experience I am ready to state without fear or favour that the only truly satisfactory point from which to watch a football match is where the hard-core fans position themselves: on the terraces behind the opposition's goal. For there can be nothing more enjoyable for the partisan spectator than being behind the enemy's goal when the ball slams into the back of the net.

Am I saying, you may wonder, that all my years in self-imposed exile from the terraces have been an entire waste of time? Not a bit of it – for there is much more to a football club than what takes place on its playing park.

'For instance, what?' you may ask.

'Well, clubroom comfort, for one thing,' I reply. 'And boardroom grub, for another.'

I have an influential friend who hails from the north, a successful man who is accepted into every Football League club at boardroom level.

'Where are you off to this week?' I asked him not long ago. 'Are you bound for the battle of the giants at White Hart Lane?' He gave me a shake of his head. 'Then perhaps you are hurrying across to QPR in order to wonder at the incredible Stan Bowles?'

'Not so,' replied my influential friend, 'I'm going over to Luton Town.'

'To see a reserve team game?' I murmured, amazed Surely there's a better fixture to be had on such a Saturday as this?'

'The match might not be the most attractive, but Luton is a very friendly club,' demurred my chum. 'And its boardroom pork-pie is the best to be had in the south of England.'

With which, he tipped his hat and scurried away to catch his train.

Well, after much careful consideration, I have come to the opinion that my itinerant acquaintance has a very good point. After all, there comes a time in every man's life when he arrives at the decision that good football alone is not everything. Good food and good companionship are of equal importance at the very least.

And so, for the benefit of sporting *bon vivants* and football's gastronomes everywhere, I have decided to publish the *GBG*.

THE GOOD BOARDROOM GUIDE

The *Good Boardroom Guide* will be an invaluable hardback publication, hopefully launched early next season, without any acknowledgement whatsoever to Egon Ronay, and loosed on to the market by that old and well-established firm of book-publishers to the gourmet trade, Messrs Hardaker & Croker Ltd, whose previous publications include: *TV Supper Snacks* by J. Hill and S. Leitch, and *Cake Icing and Decoration* by Peter Storey.

As an appetizer to the appearance in the bookshops of the long-awaited and much-overdue *Good Boardroom*

Guide, I append below a few examples from its list of contents:

★★★★ARSENAL: By far the finest epicurean treat for travelling football directors and their guests. The speciality *de la maison* at this elegant Highbury restaurant is the hot food that is ever available. Tasty sizzling sausages are *de rigueur* in this fashionable eating-place where Monsieur Hill-Wood, the *Maître d'*, presides over an excellent kitchen (ask to be shown round). Our representative tells us that, on occasion, he has dined off lamb chops and cream cakes at this *bon vivant's* delight – though this may prove to be the exception rather than the rule.

★★★★ASTON VILLA: A gastronome's idea of heaven! The boardroom setting is opulent, the food more than equal to the décor. The Villa Park boardroom may be geographically provincial, but the food provided is nothing less than capital! Do not leave without sampling the exquisite *canapes* served on silver salvers.

****CHELSEA: Brian Mears, popular restaurateur at this fashionable eating-house close by the King's Road, apologizes for any inconvenience suffered during the present renovations, but assures the clientele of his personal best attentions. Try the stuffed celery, always on the menu and a gourmand's delight unique to Stamford Bridge.

***LUTON TOWN: A warm atmosphere in this modern well-lit boardroom is matched by its pleasant homely fare, which is abundant and attractively served. Ask to sample the half-time hot soup and do not come away without tasting the pork-pie (highly recommended).

***LEICESTER CITY: A well-kept and substantial table of cold meats and fresh pastries. And if Luton Town serves the best pork-pie in the south of England, then Leicester may lay claim to providing the best pork-pie in the country. Our Midlands representative informs us that the pork-pie at this Filbert Street eating-place is delivered on match-days fresh from Melton Mowbray.

**LEEDS UNITED: Somewhat of a disappointment this Elland Road boardroom, which our informant found cramped and the food ordinary. However, the club is granted a two-star rating for its display of silverware, well-worth the trip alone, also we have been told, for what it's worth, that Leeds lays on one of the best cups of tea in football.

**SOUTHAMPTON: An unpretentious, rather sedate, yet spacious boardroom where the club's directors' ladies dispense hospitality, buttered buns and tasty triangular brown-bread sandwiches with all the olde-worlde courtesy of a Georgian tea-room.

**PORTSMOUTH: Two stars, but also a black mark for this small but popular southern boardroom. Our area representative south of London informs us that on the day that he dined here the visiting officials descended upon the table like 'a plague of locusts'. When the locusts had moved on, our correspondent was left with nothing more to choose from than 'a plate of biscuits and a morsel of seed-cake'.

*ST ALBANS CITY: An unassuming little committee room which gains a one-star rating not just because it happens to be my local club, but because it offers a unique taste sensation: ask to sample the ginger wine. I am able to let you in on a closely guarded secret. We once employed a team manager who was addicted to ginger wine and consequently the club stocked up on it. When the manager left us for pastures new, we found we had bottles and bottles of the sickly stuff on our hands, which we then laid down. Because of this circumstance, we are the only club that I know of that can offer its visitors vintage ginger wine – although, this mature and distinctive drink apart, the club's other offerings of cheese, egg or fish-paste sandwiches are nothing out of the ordinary.

Well, there it is, a foretaste of a major gastronomic literary work as yet unpublished. And you must admit that it has rare possibilities. Mark you, the volume is by no means complete, there is much work yet to be done, there are still many clubs to be visited by our representatives. So why not become one of my little band of roving gourmet reporters? Write and let me know about the nosh that's being dished up in your club's boardroom.

WARNING: The fact that you present yourself at the directors' entrance to your Football League club and announce that you are a representative of the *Good Boardroom Guide* will not *automatically guarantee* your admittance.

18 STORMY WEATHER

I was an unwilling conscript last Saturday into the ranks of soccer's missing millions. It all began at a quarter-past-ten in the morning when the phone rang in the living-room.

'Answer that,' I said to my wife. 'It might be bad news.'

I am blessed with a sort of sixth sense about these things. An official from St Albans City FC was ringing to let me know that the bad weather had beaten us and our game was off. It takes time for such horrendous tidings to sink in and I sat down for a few minutes to regain my equilibrium. I am told I went a pale shade of grey.

'You don't *have* to go to football *every* Saturday,' proffered my missis. 'Stop at home and watch sport on television.'

It seemed like a good idea for about ten minutes and then my nerve cracked. I stopped biting my finger-nails long enough to say, 'I'll ring up and see if the Luton game is on. I can nip over there quite easily.'

I telephoned Eric Morecambe, a football chum of long-standing, but it was his wife who spoke at the other end. 'Eric isn't answering the phone,' said Mrs Morecambe, 'in case it's bad news.'

Eric must have a sort of sixth sense as well – Luton's game was also cancelled, later that morning.

'You really don't have to go to football *every* Saturday,' repeated my wife.

Didn't she realize that she was speaking to a man who once flew to Dusseldorf to watch a pre-season friendly between two less-than-average German clubs because it was the close season in English football?

'I know I don't,' I replied between gritted teeth. 'I'll just stay home and watch sport on "the box".' About ten minutes later I was experiencing severe withdrawal symptoms: I was having difficulty in breathing and my finger-ends were trembling violently. 'Actually,' I said, 'I could get over to Walton and Hersham in time for their Amateur Cup encounter with Bishop's Stortford.' But another quick phone call informed me that one more possible fixture was also unavailable. I hazarded to myself that it just wasn't going to be my day. 'I think I might give football a miss this week,' I opined, trying to sound casual. 'I think I'll just stay home and watch sport on TV.'

And, having taken the decision, I was quite looking forward to it by midday.

At twelve-thirty which is when it all starts to happen on 'the box', I had browbeaten my two lads into silence (no mean feat), and organized my wife into providing me with a sort of indoor picnic lunch – devil take TV snacks! I had also surrounded myself with all the accoutrement and paraphernalia that seemed necessary for the afternoon ahead: two daily newspapers folded open at their racing pages; a notebook and pencil for jotting down selections; a telephone at my elbow providing a hot-line to the bookmaker's; both of the current weekly television journals.

I was determined of one thing at least, I wasn't going to *stir* from the comfort of my armchair until after the Classified Results at 4.45.

Well, one lives and learns.

The most irritating aspect about Saturday Sport on TV I was quickly to discover, was the way that I had to spend the entire afternoon darting back and forth, like a minnow in a jam-jar, switching from BBC to Commercial and back again to Auntie. For, from the very moment that the first decision is taken to go for either *World of*

Sport on ITV, or *Grandstand* on BBC, the viewer will
sit gnawing at his lower lip, convinced in his own mind
that while he is enduring Cyclo-Cross or the Ladies'
Uphill Slalom on his chosen Channel, a sporting event of
breath-taking excitement and earth-shattering consequence is happening at that very moment on the other
side.

It's all in the mind, of course.

In point of fact, both Channels kick-off for the afternoon with their own brand of football magazine, and you
pays your money and you takes your choice. The main
difference between ITV's *On The Ball* and BBC's
Football Preview would seem to be sartorial. Either you
prefer the elegant suitings, suggesting boardroom inside
information, of Dickie Davies and Brian Moore, or you
opt for the sports-jacketed bonhomie, indicating a close
association with Football Club terraces, as favoured by
Frank Bough and Sam Leitch. Adding up the number of
re-run goals that both programmes contrive to slip into
their schedules, there isn't much to choose between
them entertainment-wise. In fact, positioning myself at
the TV set and juggling the programme selection buttons
adroitly, albeit feverishly, I was able to watch upwards of
fifty goals slamming or slipping into the netting, leaving
upwards of fifty goalkeepers with egg upon their faces.

And upwards of fifty goals in half an hour is value for
money whichever way you look at it.

But if Saturday Sport on television augurs well from
its football magazine programmes, it tends to get worse
and worse steadily as the afternoon wears on – particularly if you manage to back the first three losers. By a
quarter-past-two last Saturday I was six quid down and
I had also sat through: Squash Rackets from Sheffield;
various ladies on ski slopes; the international incident
between Greig and Kallicharran for the umpteenth time;
and 'Cloughie' popping briefly into shot to pontificate
and emphasize his hot tip for the weekend – 'It's *very*
simple to explain as far as *I'm* concerned *why* Manchester

United will *beat* Leeds this afternoon. . . .' As it turned out, Leeds triumphed by two goals to nil. Tough luck, Brian, nobody wins them all: not you, not Manchester United, and least of all me. By two-thirty last Saturday afternoon I had retired from I T V's racing programme completely and was concentrating on the B B C.

By a stroke of good luck, another minority sport on Channel One – would you believe *Canoeing*? – sent me scurrying back to the Wolverhampton Race meeting on Commercial, and straight on to Silkstone, a 7–2 winner. It wasn't just the canoeing that got up my nostrils, it was the Beeb's sportscaster near *Come Dancing* approach to commentating: 'And here comes heading for white water – John tells me that in private life he's in the whole-sale confectionery trade with his father. . . .'

Still, from six quid in arrears I was now a oncer (less tax) in profit.

But Dame Fortune was not to favour me much longer – by three o'clock my afternoon of Telly Sport had deteriorated into a state of total chaos.

I was trying to watch *The John Player Rugby League Final* from Wigan and, at the same time, listen to the half-time results on *Sports on 2* on the radio. I wasn't having much luck. I have not yet discovered an easy way of locating *1500m* on a Japanese transistor with a dial that only goes up to 150. All I could get on the transistor was the Hertfordshire police panda cars and Eddie Waring's commentary from the box – 'Yes, he is, he's going for an up-and-under!' – was vying with an official police announcement of serious flooding on the A1 near Hatfield. While I was shaking my transistor violently, my two lads (then four and seven years old respectively), started to brawl between themselves about the distribu-tion of their *Lego* pieces. Simultaneously, the dogs, a dalmatian and a whippet, took it into their heads to savage each other behind the sofa. At which point, my wife popped her head in to announce that two gentlemen had arrived to repair the washing-machine – by the sound that was coming up from the kitchen it seemed as if they had already succeeded.

I surrendered meekly not long after and retired to my study with the portable telly. But eight inches of black-and-white screen particularly one that suffers a permanent snow-storm, is poor substitute for the luxury of twenty-four inches of living colour. Besides, I can't get BBC on the portable, and ITV had already been taken over by *Wrestling from Winslade*, a sport that seems to be primarily aimed at sex-hungry middle-aged ladies.

I never did get to see the *Classified Results*. By the time I returned to the living-room the lads were watching a children's programme, *Playaway*, on BBC2. My requests to switch over to BBC1 or ITV were hotly turned down.

'It isn't fair! We always watch *Playaway* on Saturdays, you *always* go to football.'

I didn't have the heart to argue. Actually, to be truthful, I quite enjoyed *Playaway*.

I shall be at football next Saturday, come hell or more high water. And if ever flooding causes the cancellation of every fixture in the country, I am still prepared – I'm provisionally booked on a flight to Dusseldorf where I shall watch an interesting friendly.

19 PEOPLE

THE GOALKEEPER   1974

I was reading somewhere recently that Dave Sexton's
all-time hero, and presumably ideal embryo footballer, is
the cold and inscrutable knight in the Japanese film, *The
Seven Samurai,* the one that is the total professional
dedicated to his craft who eats, sleeps, breathes and lives
solely for the purpose of perfecting his personal skills
and pursuing his chosen calling.

I have news for Mr Sexton. The man he idolizes is
alive and well and living in Leicestershire. His name is
Peter Shilton, and if Akira Kurosawa ever gets around
to making a feature film in this country he would do well
to consider the Stoke City goalkeeper as a possible
English folk-hero.

Shilton's dedication is on a par with his size. He
cruises across a hotel foyer with all the easy gait, agile
girth, and ingenuous charm of Yogi-Bear in search of a
picnic basket – on the football field, between the posts
to the opposing forwards, that same bulk is just about as
prepossessing as the proverbial brick-built karsey-wall.

Standing at just over six foot, he tips the scales at
thirteen stone eight pounds; and one gets the distinct
impression that he had nominated when he was nine
years old the exact height and weight that he would
eventually attain. One feels that nothing is ever allowed
to happen to Peter Shilton purely by chance. Certainly,
or so the story goes, as a boy he was somewhat worried
about his rate of growth and, in order to speed up the
natural process, he would hang for long periods by his
hands from the banister rails. There is another story

too, that when he opted for this peculiar and purely personal way of putting on inches, his family was living in a bungalow – it became necessary for his parents to move house in order that their young son could hang suspended by his finger-nails between two floors.

In fact, it is difficult to select legend from truth in the Peter Shilton story. He is twenty-five years old and already he is legend himself in his own city. Shilton is a Leicester lad by birth, and, when he played for Leicester, his success seemed somehow to be shared by the Leicester populace, almost in its entirety.

We are standing in a bar together when he is approached by an obsequious middle-aged stranger. 'Excuse-me-Mr-Peter-Shilton,' the man gabbles out a flood of words, 'You-are-on-the-football-field-I-am-not-on-the-football-field-and-I-know-you-but-you-do-not-know-me-and-I-would-like-to-buy-you-a-drink.' Shilton smiles at the man and courteously turns down the offer. The man rambles on for some minutes, revealing only the usual lack of football knowledge that strangers in bars are wont to do, but Shilton listens attentively, hearing him out. At the end of the totally one-sided and uninspired conversation, it seems as if the man has suddenly become aware of his own verbosity and is half-embarrassed. He excuses himself and then, before he leaves, he satisfies a need to touch his hero on the sleeve. And while it is by no means unusual for total strangers to accost famous footballers in bars, grown men approach Peter Shilton with the awe and wonder that one normally associates with urchins and autograph-hunting schoolboys.

It is curious to recollect that only a mere seven years have passed since the then seventeen-year-old Leicester City reserve goalkeeper, with only five first team games to his credit, strolled into his manager's office and said that he was 'not happy' at playing second fiddle to Gordon Banks. Those of us not in the know were half-amused at the time, and smiled to ourselves at what seemed at the time a fine example of crassly cocksure youth. Then, when it was 'Banksie's' name that went up on the transfer list, we could only wonder for the manager's sanity. And how wrong we were.

Shilton's association with Leicester City though went back much further than those seven years. In fact, he enjoyed a relationship with the club that dated back as far as 1960. When he was ten years old, Peter Shilton took a 'proficiency test' in football, organized by his primary school, through which he met George Dewis, who was on the coaching staff at Leicester, under the management of Matt Gillies. At twelve years of age, Shilton signed schoolboy forms with the club and, at fifteen, apprentice forms. It was during these formative years that the guidance and coaching of Dewis, he believes, helped him most in his career. He does not consider that he gained a lot from his role of being Number Two to Gordon Banks, not because he does not respect his predecessor but because, as he himself points out: 'Gordon was with the first team squad, I was with the reserves – I very rarely saw him *play* let alone learn anything from him.' And, 'All goalkeepers are individualists – goalkeepers don't learn a lot from other goalkeepers.' What he does admit, however, is that it was Banks' presence in the Leicester goal that drove him on to greater efforts with his own endeavours. Gordon Banks then, was the spur and not the mentor.

He organizes his own training programme – which is not an entirely unknown arrangement for a goalkeeper – but Shilton pursues his own torturous schedule with all the dedication of a medieval monk heaven-bent on self-scourging. One is left with the impression that the only cause for concern that his manager may ever have, is that the player may be driving himself too hard in training; a worry that many managers today might wish to come across more often.

It occurred to Shilton, about two years ago, that what he needed was something new in his training schedule to give him just that final honing to his already 100 per cent physical sharpness. He took himself off, forthwith, to his local army recruiting centre.

I sympathized with him. Alas, I had made the same mistake myself when I was a raw-boned lad and had spent seven years of my life regretting the visit.

In Peter Shilton's case, however, if the British Army did not entirely recruit a world-class goalkeeper, at least it made a convert to its physical training programmes.

The Stoke City keeper now trains, on average, once a week at a Signals Training Centre in Leicestershire. He begins his day on the army assault course and then jogs back to the gymnasium where he pursues a rigid and well-organized schedule of exercises, a light-weights circuit, and finishes off his session on a trampoline. Naturally, it has been his assault course antics that have gained him the most publicity. But he is inclined to shrug off this addendum to his life-style as though suffering an army assault course was as natural a way of kicking off a Monday morning as TV commercials claim is the Sunshine Breakfast.

He is full of praise for his army Physical Training Instructor, Sergeant-Major 'Jock' Scott, who not only organizes but also personally supervises Shilton's mornings with the army. And while he is quick to insist that he believes ball-work to be the most important part of his training, he feels that the added edge he gains in fitness by pursuing his army sessions makes it a hair's-breadth second.

His team-mates were wont at first to look slightly askance at his military high-jinks – regarding them as the somewhat suspect cranky behaviours to which goalkeepers are considered prone – but they have been having second thoughts. In recent months, more than one of his fellow-players has been observed tackling the army's assault course of their own accord.

All goalkeepers, the saying goes, are barmy. Without doubt they are all committed individualists. And why should committed individualists choose to devote themselves to a team sport? Because they are goalkeepers and because, in part, all goalkeepers are barmy. I once knew a goalkeeper who was only completely happy when he was playing himself at golf. There's a message in that somewhere.

Peter Shilton is the shining example of the man who believes that practice makes perfect. His interests outside of football are minimal. While he is willing to supplement his income by lending his name to a couple of brand products, he steadfastly refuses to involve himself in any personal business ventures. He belongs implacably to that much-to-be-admired but sadly fast-diminishing band of top-grade athletes who maintain that no sportsman can give of his absolute best unless his life is totally committed to the game.

Shilton's requirements for his personal contentment are deceptively simple – he needs to keep goal immaculately in a team that equals in performance the standards that he sets himself.

Peter Shilton's private life is as impeccable as his goalkeeping. Not for him the bright lights and London's night-club champagne lure. He has even eschewed the simpler sodium-glare of provincial evenings for a house in the country and village life. He gives the impression of having all that he needs. He has an extremely pretty wife and he has a young son and he is plainly devoted to both. He is without hobbies. He has a large garden in which he 'potters about', not because he likes gardening but because he 'likes things tidy'. Well, why not? He keeps a very tidy goal.

He has one main ambition: to be voted European Footballer of the Year. And if an incredible sufficiency of skill and a self-imposed commitment of total dedication are the attributes that are required to achieve that honour, then he will probably get that too.

'*Blimey, you wouldn't think it was the same
bleeding match . . .*'

1974

THE COMMENTATOR

Among the stronger of my childhood memories are those
I have of the pre-war Rugby League Challenge Cup
Finals at Wembley Stadium – probably because I never
managed to get to any of them.

My father went though, every year, along with the rest
of the men in our street – every street was a Coronation
Street in those carefree days. For months and months
before the actual event, while the womenfolk sniffed, the
men put away their sixpences like diligent squirrels,
saving up the 15s. 6d. return fare by rail to London. In
those impecunious times, the fans travelled down

through the Friday night in order to save unnecessary expense on such frivolities as hotel bills and thus bump up their beer money. It was also intended that they should travel back to the north on the Saturday night, but they rarely did. Saturday nights were reserved for carousing and rampaging through the London streets. It was rumoured in Leeds that there was one particular pub in London, and only one, that served Tetley's bitter beer – my father spent his one weekend in the capital, year after fruitless year, in search of that one particular pub with the same dedicated perseverance that Round Table Knights observed when they sought the Holy Grail. And although my old man never found his famous boozer, it didn't really matter, for on his journeys he saw much of London life and got more than his share of London beer.

The men returned to their homes late on Sunday nights, overdue on their privileged passes, the womenfolk sniffed louder than ever and, in our house at least, the female ostracized the male for several days. They had returned like Greeks, bearing unattractive and unlikely gifts which they had bought, or so they claimed, in a street market with the improbable name of Petticoat Lane which was open, or so they said, on Sunday mornings. And the womenfolk sniffed even louder still, for they knew for certain fact that there was no such thing as a Sunday market.

Well, that's how it was in my young days. Little, it seems, has changed over the years.

For the men from the north, the Rugby League Challenge Cup Final is still the event that it was in my childhood days. For while it may still be overshadowed in importance by the FA Cup, it somehow contrives to remain a friendlier occasion, a more intimate affair, than its posh soccer relative.

For one thing, the Rugby League Challenge Cup Final has always been first and foremost a jaunt – a trip, a weekend out, two days on the loose. It is as much a part of the northern scene as mushy peas, trundle pies, polony, black pudding and Eddie Waring.

Indeed, for those that also serve, who only stay at home and wait and watch it on the box, Eddie Waring *is* the Rugby League Challenge Cup Final – for the very idea of a Rugby League Final *without* Eddie Waring's commentary is entirely unthinkable.

Eddie – it is impossible to think of him as *Waring* – came of age as a television commentator in 1974 when, believe it or not, he entertained many, and infuriated some, with his 21st Rugby League Challenge Cup Final broadcast.

And how many of soccer's famed commentators with their carefully enunciated screams and their rallying-call of '*That's* what soccer's all about!' have come and gone over the past couple of decades? Well, Eddie is with us still, and *that's* what Rugby League is all about and, what's more, he looks like hanging on to his microphone for many years to come. There is no heir apparent to the 'Up-and-Under' throne. For while soccer today has got its David Colemans, its Jimmy Hills, its Brian Moores, its Frank Boughs, its Sam Leitchs *et al.*; Rugby League has got its Eddie Waring who is its commentator, its reporter, its analyst, its sportscaster – you name it, Eddie's it.

There is, it seems, some slight area of contention about which was the first-ever Rugby League game to be televised in the north. Pints are wagered upon the answer in Wigan, bets are struck in pickled walnuts throughout Wakefield pubs. And Eddie is ever-ready to come up with the correct answer. He carries a phenomenal computer-bank of Rugby League facts in his head and, in fact, handles a question-and-answer newspaper column called *Ask Eddie* in the Sunday press.

'Yes, it's an interesting question is that,' he says with relish and a slow smile for, being a Yorkshireman, there is nothing he likes so much as a poser that promises a little bit of *argy-bargy*. 'The first ever Rugby League game that was televised on the national network was the 1951 Test Match between Great Britain and New Zealand,' and he pauses for effect. '*But* the previous year the BBC televised the Rugby League Challenge Cup Final between Warrington and Widnes on the Midland Region only.' I proffered that it still seemed a pretty straightforward question, but Eddie produced his *argy-bargy* content with all the natural-born enthusiasm of a Dewsbury man. 'Yer see, although the Warrington–Widnes final was a Midland Regional programme, it was picked up by freak reception in certain parts of Lancashire. . . .'

It would seem that when the question crops up in Wigan the arguers end up paying for their own pints; when it is asked in Wakefield then the collier-lads are left meditatively sucking on pickled walnuts they have paid for themselves. Eddie offered further to fill me in off the top of his head with both of the match results, the size of the crowds, and the gate receipts, but I surrendered quietly.

Not many people realize – I hadn't known for one – that Eddie Waring had once been a Rugby League club manager, firstly with Dewsbury and later with Leeds. And before that, he was a player himself.

He graduated from Rugby League management into Rugby League journalism gradually. He is proud of the fact that he was one of the first three sports journalists to travel on an Australian Rugby League Tour. He sailed on the Aircraft Carrier Indomitable in 1946 when, in the words of sports editor, George Casey, 'Two tons of rugby sailed for Australia.' His subsidized fare on that first occasion, which again he recalls with his infinite love for detail, was £11 11s. 2d., and which he paid himself. It was the first, and remains the only, tour of Australia in which the British Tourists never lost a match.

Again with total recall, Eddie will tell you that his shipboard companions on the voyage – that two ton of rugby apart – were returning Royal Australian Air Force officers and a party of thirty-six priests. The outward-bound final of the deck hockey competition was played out between the Wigan Wallopers and a team of priests. The priests won. 'Those priests,' he muses, 'played the dirtiest game of anything I've ever seen.'

There have been eight Test Tours of Australia since the one of '46, and Eddie Waring has been on every one of them.

Apart from the Rugby League Challenge Cup Final coverage, the BBC also screened during the 1973/74 season: six Saturday afternoon second-half cup ties; twelve forty-five minute sessions of the Floodlit Cup on BBC2; the second halves of the sixth round of the John Player Cup; the second halves of the semi-finals and the final of the Captain Morgan Cup; some half dozen league games and two Saturday afternoon seven-a-side competitions. Eddie Waring provided the commentary for all of them.

The faithful Eddie Waring fans, and they are legion, will insist that he cannot put a plummy northern vowel wrong. There is an *Eddie Waring Appreciation Society* at

Liverpool University, there is another that styles itself *The Official Eddie Waring Appreciation Society* at Lanchester Polytechnic, which devotes itself to charitable works by way of 'Up and Under' parties and Annual Fuddles. The Liverpool lot appeared on the BBC's Nationwide programme, doing various impersonations of Eddie. He found the idea amusing, but summed it up modestly, 'Of course, they weren't really doing imitations of me – they were doing imitations of Mike Yarwood imitating me.' Mike Yarwood's imitation of Eddie Waring is one of Mike Yarwood's funniest imitations.

The Eddie Waring detractors, and there are quite a few of them too, have been known to shout and stamp and tear their hair whenever his rich voice-over commentaries assault their ear-drums.

Their main complaint, it seems, is that Eddie has the audacity to treat Rugby League football as if it were a *game!* Why, they rant, can't he treat it *seriously?*

Well, one of the nice things about Rugby League is that in many ways it still *is* a game. All Rugby League players are part-timers who are paid, on average, about fifteen pounds a week, plus small win bonuses – which is a darn sight less than many of soccer's privileged shamateurs are getting. And as long as Rugby League remains a part-time profession, devoid of the big-business big-money payments that have turned soccer into a bone-shattering industry, the longer it will remain a game, and long may it continue to do so. As a matter of interest, the Warrington players in the '73/74 Challenge Cup Final at Wembley were on a forty-five pound per man win bonus – compare that with the bonuses that soccer's Wembley finalists were on, and then pause to wonder.

The other point is, of course, that Eddie Waring *does* take Rugby League seriously – after all, it is his living – but not *too* seriously. And there are far too many of soccer's self-styled analysts and commentators who are taking their particular brand of football so seriously that they are beginning to drive me personally to both distraction and old movies on the other channel. Television's soccer coverage is starting to take on all the immediacy, urgency and excitement of a recorded mathematics lecture. And whatever the criticisms that are levelled at Eddie Waring, he can never be accused of being *boring*.

His Saturday afternoon audiences are upwards of six million – and rising steadily. He has succeeded in introducing a northern game to a southern audience, and made it interesting. And if the complaint is made that while he has raised his audience's interest, he has never gone out of his way to explain the rules of the game, he will reply: 'I could teach twenty-two aborigines the basic rules of soccer in half an hour, it would take me half a day to teach them just to form a scrum.' He has a point, undoubtedly.

Apart from his Rugby League life, and in case anybody isn't aware of the fact, he is not unconnected with a BBC show called *It's A Knockout* which has also swept aside European TV barriers, boundaries and viewing figures under its *nomme de guerre: Jeux Sans Frontières*. He has also been known to introduce a TV programme of religious ditties called *Songs of Praise*. He has done the obligatory radio show for celebrities, *Desert Island Discs*, and he has appeared *with* Mike Yarwood as well as being imitated by him. He has been seen on *The Goodies*. But he received the highest accolade of show business when he joined those illustrious ranks that include Sir Laurence Olivier, Glenda Jackson, Andre Previn, Rudolph Nureyev and Dame Flora Robson, to name but a few, who have been invited to do a guest appearance on the *Morecambe and Wise Show*.

I am one of those that makes his annual pilgrimage to Wembley for the Rugby League Challenge Cup Final, even though my own team, Hunslet, seldom seem to figure in the official proceedings. In fact, the only time that Hunslet have made Wembley during my supporting days was in 1966 when, alas, I was stuck in Hollywood

working on a film script. I remember that I waited by
the news-stand on the corner of Hollywood Boulevard
and Vine Street, for the arrival of the flimsy airmail
papers. Then, when they did turn up, I read to my
dismay that Hunslet had gone down to Wigan by 16 points
to 20.

And I took myself off to a hamburger joint on the
Sunset Strip where I drowned my sorrows in Pepsi-
Colas and munched doughnuts disconsolately. And it
wasn't *just* Hunslet that I was sad about, even though it
was reading about the match that brought on my misery.
For suddenly, in that hot Californian afternoon, I had
become a lonely man from the north of England who was
homesick for all of his natural rights like mushy peas and
trundle pies and polony and black pudding and Eddie
Waring. . . .

THE FOOTBALL MANAGER   1974
The Fourth Division football club, particularly one
which has had to see re-election, has become fair game
for many a TV playwright (myself included), and has
also replaced the mother-in-law as the favourite butt of
the comedian:

*'This fella – this fella rings up Darlington FC an' he
says, "I'm bringing a party of four to the game tonight,
what time's the kick-off?" So the geezer on the other end of
the line comes back, "What time can you get here?"'*

Or there's the one that began:

*'I say, I say, I say, my brother's joined Northampton
Town. . . .'*

Bill Dodgin Jr joined Northampton Town. He went
there at the start of the 1973–4 season, as manager, and
he took with him a track record which is the envy of
many a manager in the more salubrious divisions.

Dodgin's career on the managerial side of football
began when he joined Millwall, as coach to the then
manager, Billy Gray, for the 1965–6 season. During that
season Millwall won promotion to the Second Division.

125

At the end of 1966, Dodgin went to Queen's Park Rangers, again as coach and to Alec Stock's manager. In the 1966-7 season, QPR won the League Cup as well as promotion to the Second Division, and in the following season Rangers joined the footballing élite and went up to the First.

In November, 1968, Bill Dodgin went to Fulham where Johnny Haynes was holding uneasy sway as player–manager, a post he had accepted only on the understanding that Dodgin be allowed to join him as coach. Haynes found the manager's chair uncomfortable for his own particular aspirations, and Dodgin moved into his first managerial seat.

Fulham's star was in full descendancy that year and Dodgin, joining them when he did in the second half of the season, was unable to stop the slide to the Third Division. In the season that followed, however, he raised the morale of the playing staff and Fulham finished in a respectable position in the League. In 1970-71, Dodgin took Fulham back to the Second Division, and in the following season he kept them there.

Fulham struggled that year, and their remaining in the Second Division was dependent on their final fixture. They fought out a grim and dour battle at Craven Cottage on a mirthless Saturday afternoon and held Sunderland to a no-score draw. To be certain of missing the drop, Fulham had needed to win, and the draw necessitated that players, fans and directors alike had to wait anxiously at the ground for another result to come over the phone. It came: Charlton had lost to Blackpool, 4-1, and Fulham grinned with nervous relief. Charlton went down and Fulham stayed up.

The usual celebrations took place in the dressing-rooms and offices, and Bill Dodgin was presented by his thankful directors with football's almost obligatory accolade: a bottle of champagne. About four weeks later, and in the middle of the close season, Dodgin was handed a carbon copy of a letter informing him of his dismissal from the club. The original letter, he was told, was in the post to his home address and he was being handed the carbon in order that he shouldn't learn of his sacking from the mid-day press.

Soccer's administrative hierarchy is nothing if not considerate at all times.

Dodgin spent the 1972–3 season as coach at Leicester City, under Jimmy Bloomfield's management. When Dodgin was offered the Northampton Town job, both Bloomfield and the Leicester City board of directors were reluctant to let him go, but at the same time they had no desire to stand in the way of his ambitions.

One man who has been particularly enthusiastic about Dodgin's brand of football is soccer analyst, Jimmy Hill. It was Hill who advised Haynes to grab Dodgin as his coach at Fulham. It was also Hill who, in talks with the Northampton Town directors, advised them to approach Bill Dodgin when they were seeking a new manager.

Bill Dodgin was installed at Northampton Town; the club since then has been dedicated to clean attacking football, and the game is that much the better off for it.

But, if Bill Dodgin had arrived at a new club bringing with him an enviable record, the club itself had a unique past history of its own. Northampton Town was the first club to rise from the Fourth to the First Division, where it arrived in the mid-sixties after an illustrious journey accomplished over a mere five seasons. But Northampton slid back to the lower rungs of the Fourth Division ladder, again in record time, and remained there, alone and palely loitering, until Dodgin joined them.

The managership of a side that has just been forced to seek re-election is, to say the least, a formidable post – but the new manager accepted the job without any apparent undue trepidation. He began the season without making any sweeping changes to his playing staff.

'I am told,' he said, 'by people at Northampton whose judgement I respect, that the lads were playing better football before I came than their league position justified.

I'm prepared to go along with that belief unless events prove otherwise.'

And he did go along with the belief to the extent that he made no pre-season signings in his first year. Dodgin's show of confidence in his playing staff was rewarded by a growing confidence among the players themselves – and that confidence was given a welcome booster when, in their first league game, they beat newly demoted Rotherham.

Some measure of the difficulties facing a new manager at the start of a season may be judged by the fact that of the fifteen league clubs which began the season with a new man in charge of the team, only two were successful in their first league fixture: Jack Charlton at Middlesbrough was one, the other was Bill Dodgin – Charlton's continued phenomenal success in his first season is now legend; Dodgin was also successful in that he succeeded in lifting Northampton from the foot of the Fourth Division up to one run from promotion.

For a club that had had to fight so hard for so little return over recent past seasons, there was a marked lack of tension in the Northampton Town dressing-room at the start of Dodgin's reign. And this is part and parcel of the man's approach to the game.

'There are managers,' he says, 'who go out of their way to create dressing-room tensions before a match, but it's my belief that the game itself creates tensions enough.'

One of the major obstacles in taking over a Fourth Division side, Dodgin was quickly to discover, was that of inheriting a totally unknown quantity with regard to the talent available at the club.

'When you join a club in the First or Second Division, you know more or less immediately what you are taking on. You've a good idea of the players' capabilities and individual talents – you've watched their performances, if not on the field then, at least, on television – they come to you with some sort of reputation. You may not accept that reputation, but at least it exists; it provides a yardstick by which to form your own opinion of a player's worth. When you arrive at a Fourth Division club, you find yourself with a bunch of lads whose names you've never heard of, and you have to start from scratch, assessing the different qualities of each and every one of them from square one.'

At the same time, Dodgin was to discover that this major handicap had also got its compensations:

'The satisfying thing about working with a squad of unknown youngsters is that they're keen, anxious to learn and eager to do what you tell them, both in training and during a game. Many of the so-called stars in the upper reaches of football are convinced that they know it all already and are not prepared to listen to or try out new ideas.'

Northampton Town, when Dodgin took over, *were* a young side, judged even by Fourth Division standards.

'I think it's possible that their youth was partly responsible for their lack of success before I came,' said Dodgin. 'They had a few bad results and they started to play below themselves. But, by the same principle, if a team of youngsters get off to a good start, they are apt to play above themselves.'

Confidence, say the pundits, is what football is all about. Dodgin agreed that the pundits, for once, may well be right.

'All footballers are insecure,' Dodgin told me. I said that the same thing was true of actors, and we decided that the insecurity of the individual, in both cases, sprang from employment in a basically insecure profession. And, if that is the case, then there can't be many jobs less conducive to a feeling of well-being and security than that of playing for a Fourth Division club down, down among the lower echelons.

Bill Dodgin's way with players is to cajole rather than bluster, enthuse rather than criticize.

'I watched a pre-season game this year between a First Division side and one from the Second Division,' he said.

'The Second Division team won by the odd goal in three, but the First Division team gave much the better display, and were unlucky. If I'd been the manager of the First Division bunch, I'd have gone into the dressing-room after the game and complimented the lads on their showing. In fact, the manager in question gave his team a rollicking,'

And Dodgin recounts the incident with some slight bemusement – confident of his own approach to the game, curious that another method can also bring about results.

Bill Dodgin Jr is a popular figure in football, and not only with his own players and supporters.

'When the results come in, I always look first to see how Bill's lot have got on,' is a remark I've heard expressed by many people inside the game. Good results, however, are not born of good wishes but of slogging hard work and a modicum of good luck.

Northampton Town, under Dodgin's sway, have put in the hard work and are being rewarded with their just share of the 'run-of-the-ball'.

Slowly, in that first season, they hoisted themselves from the bottom of the Division, rung by rung, to a respectable position – and there is nothing more difficult in football than picking oneself up from off the floor. They have made a more than workmanlike start, without being flamboyant – but then there is nothing flamboyant about their manager who views the club's future, and his own, with his personal brand of dour and cautious optimism.

One thing is certain – since the arrival of Bill Dodgin, the comedians have stopped telling jokes about Northampton Town.

THE CHAIRMAN   1974

'What's *your* name, laddie?'

The recently enrolled aircraftsman trembled on the Padgate drill square as he felt the inspecting NCO's chill breath on his left ear.

'Mears, sir,'

'*Sergeant.*'

'Mears, sergeant.'

'Mears. . .? Mears. . .?' and the sergeant's voice perked up with interest. 'I've heard that name before You wouldn't, by any remote chance, be related to *Joe* Mears?'

'Yes, sergeant. He's my father.'

'You couldn't, by any remote possibility, manage to get me any Cup Final tickets, I don't suppose?'

It was 1951, and it occurred then to Brian Mears that, even in uniform, it helped to have the Chairman of a League Football Club for a father. Certainly his own two-year burden of National Service showed signs of being made a little lighter.

The history of the Mears' family association with Chelsea Football Club dates back as far as the team's conception, for it was Brian's great-uncle, Gus Mears, who formed the club in 1905. Gus Mears had bought the area of land at Stamford Bridge for £3,000 the previous year and had offered it to Fulham Football Club. Fulham were not interested in the proposition, and Gus, nothing loth, decided to put together his own football club. With the assistance of his brother – would you believe, Theophilus? – Gus organized the laying of a football field, the building of a stadium, the enlistment of a board of directors, the assembling of a playing staff; and he named this conglomeration that was his brain-child, Chelsea Football Club. It just so happened, in those easy-go-lucky days of the Football League's existence, that there was a vacancy in the Second Division and Chelsea's application, coincidentally ideally timed, fitted neatly into the League's empty pigeon-hole. Augustus and Theophilus, both prosperous builders in their working lives, were content to sit back on the Chelsea board of directors and watch their sporting venture prosper.

Two generations later, Brian Mears, at forty-three, is in the Chairman's well-padded seat at Chelsea Football

Club, and his great-uncle's £3,000 investment has turned into a multi-million business proposition.

It seems curious, in these commerce-ridden times that we live in, how little is known by football supporters about the role that is played in their club by the chairman, or the extent to which the chairman influences a club's success or failure. Good chairman tend to beaver away behind the scenes in football, unnoticed – like good referees they are at their best when the paying public is unaware of their existence. Consequently, their function at a club is often misinterpreted by the supporters who are inclined to mistrust not only chairmen but all directors, and consider the difference between the board and the playing staff as being the same as that that exists in industry between management and labour. Such false analogy may well be accentuated at a 'family' club like Chelsea with its 'trouble-at-t'-mill' sounding lineage:

'*And there was Augustus Mears whose brother Theophilus begat Joseph Mears who begat Brian Mears. . . .*'

Joe was the first of the Mears' to accept the chairmanship of the club, a post he held from 1940 until his death in 1966. He involved himself in the game more deeply than his father or his uncle had before him; his was a passionate dedication to football and he was – and for that matter is still regarded as – one of a very few boardroom figures that gained the respect and admiration of the crowds on the terraces. Joe Mears was keen to instil in his son a similar love for football.

Brian Mears recalls the first time that he was taken to Stamford Bridge by his father to watch Chelsea play. It was back in 1945, Brian was thirteen years old, and the Blues' opponents that day were the visiting Moscow Dynamos. He remembers now that the thing that impressed him most was the size of the crowd that was jam-packed in at the Bridge that afternoon. He had never before seen so many people assembled together in the same place at the same time and, peering over the edge of the directors' box, his eyes were inclined to stray from the action on the pitch.

'Is it like this every week?' he inquired of his father in hushed tones.

'Shut up and watch the game,' was the peremptory reply.

Brian, being an obedient lad, did as he had been told – and he has been watching the game ever since.

The track record of Brian Mears, the avid Chelsea supporter, is an impressive one. Since his appointment to the Board of Directors, fifteen years ago, he reckons that he can count on the fingers of one hand the first team games he has missed, home or away – and he is inclined to mention those few occasions ruefully.

Mears succeeded his father as Chelsea chairman in 1966, since when his involvement with the running of the club's affairs has become a six-day a week commitment. And just for the sake of clarifying an often misunderstood situation: Football League secretaries are paid servants of their clubs; League chairmanships are entirely honorary appointments.

Brian Mears spends every morning, Monday to Friday, in his office at Stamford Bridge, and his weekday afternoons are devoted to his various business obligations: he is also the chairman of an advertising company, the director of a shipping firm, and he has an interest in a garaging business. And while he will readily acknowledge that there are advantages to be gained from being on he inside of soccer, business contacts, for example – football's boardrooms have a near masonic cliquishness – the will also argue that benefits thus gained are outweighed by the time-consuming propensities of soccer chairmanship. He could well have a point. Unpaid offices in any organization are apt to snowball insidiously on their holder. And, in addition to holding the chairmanship of Chelsea, Brian Mears can also count himself: a member of the FA Council; a member of the FA Disciplinary Committee; a member of the FA Challenge Cup

Committee – all of which bodies hold regular meetings and all of which meetings he makes a point of attending.

He is also a council member of the *Goaldiggers*, a charitable organization which, in the words of Prince Philip, the Goaldiggers coach, 'exists to provide football pitches and play-areas where children and young people can, amongst other things, kick a ball about in safety.' And as a fellow council member myself of the same organization, I am well aware of the time that alone takes up.

On top of all of which, Brian Mears makes a point of attending as many of Chelsea's reserve and youth team games as he can possibly fit in. 'It's good for the morale of the younger players,' he will tell you, and: 'They like to know that one of the directors is watching them.' Which is no doubt true, but one also gets the impression that Mears likes nothing better than watching football at any level – whatever his reason or excuse.

What else?

Well, last but by no means least in tediousness, there are those interminable and abominable football dinners that it is thought necessary to attend.

'How many of them do you get to?' I asked him.

'About one a week on average,' he sighed, and for the first time his face showed signs of strain.

I accorded him my well-deserved sympathy. Fifty-two football dinners, by the simplest of mathematical calculations, works out at fifty-two plates of pale and insipid mushroom soup, an *awful* amount of dehydrated croquette potatoes, and vast unconsumable quantities of so-called *bombes, glacés* and *surprises*, all to be consumed.

Well, it is all in a good cause.

'Wait one moment,' says the voice of the cynic. 'What about that original £3,000 investment of old astute Augustus Mears? That must be worth a good few pence in these inflated days?'

Indeed it must. For the record book, it had escalated to £475,000 when the trustees for the Mears family sold the freehold rights to Chelsea Football Club, in 1969, in order that the club could redevelop the ground.

And the fruits of that transaction have risen over Stamford Bridge in the shape of the grand new stand, oft-times criticized in its construction days. The criticism, in the opinion of the club's chairman 'is born only out of frustration', he says, adding, 'We aren't the first club in the country to build a stand since the war – but we *are* the first club to pull down a stand in order to build a better one.'

What about the £475,000 in the Mears family bank account? Why not? Brian Clough has stated that he would like to make a million before he gives up the game. It's now close on seventy years since Gus Mears made his initial investment, and the family is still chasing one half of 'Cloughey's' proposed target.

Brian Mears would not deny that football has been good to his family – but on the other hand, the Mears family has been good for football.

Good football managers, it is said, are hard to come by; but good football club chairmen are a damn sight harder to find – and it sometimes seems a shame, to me at least, that they rarely receive their share of the plaudits.

'What do you think,' I asked Brian Mears, 'is the quality you have that is most useful to you as the Chelsea chairman?' We had downed two carafes of wine with lunch and I am inclined, I am told, towards pomposity when I have had a few.

He took the question in his stride.

'Experience,' he said.

With three generations to back his claim, and with the second double brandy arriving at the table, I was not disposed to argue.

ENGLAND'S BOSS   1974
Among the least advertised (and possibly even less enthralling) sports which take place in London is the plethora of makeshift football matches that are played in

Hyde Park every weekday afternoon. The players consist of Italian and Spanish waiters, taking a break between their luncheon and dinner duties; the football strip worn is informal as are the pitches, where an occasional soup-spotted dinner-jacket may be observed standing in for a goal-post.

Novelist and playwright, Bill Naughton, at about the age of fifty-six, was wont to take his soccer boots to Hyde Park every afternoon and hang about on the non-existent touchlines, hoping for a game. Naughton has played football all his life and he confided to me once his divine sporting ambition; 'I have always wanted, Willis, to play in a football match with *real* goalposts.'

Bill must be over sixty now, still playing football with the lads, still folding up and putting down his jacket, but he has retired to sunnier climes in search of the fulfilment of ambition.

We need not despair though. The Union Jack is kept flying in Hyde Park, for, although Naughton has gone another Englishman now dons a tracksuit and jogs alone most weekdays on the periphery of the makeshift foreign football matches. His name is Don Revie. Although he has not yet been invited to make up a side of Italian or Spanish waiters many men in this country – and I count myself among the most fervent of them – look to him as the future saviour of English international football.

The fact that he still trains each day is just part of his professional dedication although he would probably shrug it off as habit.

I met him a couple of weeks ago in Leeds, where he has kept the home he returns to at weekends, and where every other shop, it seems, is flogging souvenirs and sporting goods in tribute to the man and to the team that he brought back all those years ago from the brink of soccer obscurity.

On the station bookstall, the current issue of *Super-sportspecial* hails *Champions Leeds!* and features Don Revie, the Maker of champions – and if Maker has an almost divine ring about it, then it's very likely intentional.

'Superleeds' pottery is on sale in every china shop; the Herbert Sutcliffe Sports Shop window is full not, as its name might suggest, of cricket bats but of Leeds United jerseys in all sizes: boy's, youths' and small men's – and what would a *small* man be doing, one wonders, in a Leeds United jersey? The peel-off stick-on badges on sale in Leeds still bear Revie's craggy likeness.

I was born in Leeds myself – indeed was christened by my doting parents after one of Leeds' greatest players of the thirties – and when I make the trek back north to the city of the publicity styled 'Superchampions' if my relatives don't kill the fatted calf, at least they are inclined to crack open a cask of Tetley's bitter.

On the morning that I had arranged to meet Mr Revie, I was suffering from a 'Superhangover' and in no fit state to meet the manager of a back-street fish-and-chip shop let alone confront the manager of the England team. Not without first attempting to force down my throat a hair-of-the-dog-that-bit-me.

'If called upon,' I told a sympathetic hotel porter, 'I shall be in the bar. I am expecting a guest at twelve o'clock – it's Mr Don Revie.'

'Good God, sir, is it really?' was all that the porter could manage, goggle-eyed and breathless with excitement at the prospect.

He arrived on the stroke of the hour, looking incredibly fit, spruce and freshly showered after having just completed his dose of daily training in a local park. Declining alcohol, he settled for a glass of iced water, and the half-pint of lemonade-and-bitter shandy held insecurely in my twitching fist suddenly seemed entirely inappropriate.

We talked of football and of golf and of family ties and of the importance of being northern.

Revie's own background is the obligatory one for a football manager of his generation: the childhood upbringing in a two-up-and-two-down terrace house; the formative years spent booting a spent tennis ball against a red-brick wall . . . where is the manager of middle-age who didn't suffer it? Which gives one cause to wonder whether, in twenty years or so, we shall suffer a spate of football managers who were all brought up on the top floors of high-rise blocks of flats and idled away their boyhood hours by bashing balls against penthouse closet walls?

But if Don Revie's early days were run-of-the-embryo-manager's-mill, his life-style in the large home he now owns in one of Leeds' classier suburbs, is anything but ordinary. Together with his wife, Elsie (with whom he celebrates twenty-five years of marriage this year), he shares his house with his mother, who is eighty years of age; two aunts, Jean and Janet, seventy-nine and eighty respectively; and Uncle Willie, who clocks in at eighty-six, and thus achieves the distinction of being the senior citizen of the family.

And, as if that houseful wasn't large enough for anybody, Don and Elsie are only too delighted when their two children are home from college.

It is Revie's family, one gets the impression, that provides the chink in his armour of modesty. For if he manages to hide his pride and sound dispassionate when he talks of his own career, he warms and mellows on the theme of the family.

His son, Duncan, is at Queen's College, Cambridge, reading law; his daughter, Kim, is at Queenswood College, Hatfield studying music. Both of them are good at sport; both of them are firm followers of Leeds United – whether or not they will transfer their first allegiance to the England team would seem to be a matter of conjecture. And Revie will also tell you with a hint of pride, if somewhat ruminatively, that Elsie beats him frequently at golf, a rare admittance for a man who plays off a handicap of eight.

But it comes as no secret that Don Revie is a family man, for the family that was his creation entirely at

Elland Road was as tight-knit, as clanny, and ten times as explosive as the BBC TV's Wilkins lot. 'I did try to build a sort of family atmosphere,' he says, 'although I never met the players socially – I don't believe in it – except at get-togethers: weddings, christenings, Christmas parties, times like that. *Family* occasions.'

Revie's first team family squad of players always got together every Friday night before a match: 'Home or away, it made no difference. If it was an away game, we travelled down the night before – if we were playing at home, we spent the night in a hotel outside Ilkley. I stopped them getting too keyed up about the match by organizing Bingo games. Saturday mornings were always the same: chicken or steak, whatever they fancied, and a bingo session.'

And the family feeling he had for his players even went so far as his giving the lads their weekly soap massage himself, a Thursday ritual at Elland Road.

He needs, he says, to feel 'totally involved' with his players. 'Involvement' is a word he uses often. 'Involvement at every level now, not only with the England squad – with the Youth team, with the Under Twenty-threes.'

And how does he hope to engender his family spirit among a group of players that he will meet but rarely, eight times a year at the most? 'Regular "talk-ins" to put the squad in the picture with regard to plans and ideas, both on and off the field.'

One welcome innovation is his obvious desire to keep the media aware of, indeed *involved* with, all his plans; particularly as his predecessor's sense of persecution by the Press seemed, at times, to verge upon the manic.

Revie has begun his job as England's manager by arranging a series of press conferences from top to bottom of the country: in Sunderland, in Manchester, in Birmingham and in London – a sort of intermittent whistle-stop tour that would do credit to an unimpeachable American statesman. He says that he wants to be

'get-at-able' at all times; and if he is not in his London
FA office, then he is 'get-at-able' at his home in Leeds at
weekends.

I asked him if all of this was a deliberate policy,
formulated at the FA to improve the relations with the
press that had been in such a sad decline during the
Ramsey era? But he denied the suggestion. 'I've always
been available to talk on the 'phone – that's how it was
when I was at Leeds, it's exactly the same now.'

If it would prove the slightest benefit, one feels, he
would willingly publish his telephone number in the
personal columns of a national daily newspaper. 'I *need*
the Press to sell the England team,' he says, and means it.

It's a long hard slog to the next World Cup and, of
necessity, the lessons that were to be learned at Munich
may play but a small part in the plans of the England
team four years hence. Revie states that he 'took note of
the fact that both the Germans and the Dutch were prepared to throw men forward from the back.' The squad
that we have in four years' time will govern our own
particular tactics then.

Around fifty players were summoned to the first of the
new England manager's 'talk-ins', held at Manchester
over a two-day period last month. And which of those
summoned will be called upon to play against Czechoslovakia this month is anybody's food for argument. One
thing is certain, though – that Revie has never been
afraid to test new talent. Indeed, his willingness to back
his own judgement has always been one of his biggest
assets as a manager.

Way back in 1962, a year after his appointment as
Leeds United's manager, and when the club were just
embarking on the hazardous struggle from the lower
reaches of the Second Division, Revie experimented with
his first team to the extent of introducing four new faces
in the side in one League fixture – youngsters whose
names were Sprake, Reaney, Hunter and Johnson.

In the run-up to his first fixture as manager of the

England side, he has attended, on average, four matches every week: 'Saturday, Monday, Tuesday, Wednesday and off again on Saturday.' He has committed himself to 'seeing as many players and talking to as many managers as possible.'

His relationship with his fellow-managers he sees as being of incalculable importance. He recognizes and admits that League managers will continue, as he himself has done before, to put club before country. But he feels that if he can impress upon them that while players are under his wing, and are in need of any attention for knocks or injuries, they will be assured of the services of 'the best surgeons, the best physiotherapists, the best medical attention and equipment that there is in the country,' he will be able to count more on their co-operation.

As the seasons slide away, and the next World Cup draws nearer, Revie plans to take his England team on tour in South America in 1977, to 'try out teams and hotels and football stadiums'.

When Don Revie told me of his daily training stints, practised by himself, around Hyde Park, it seemed, somehow, a curious and complete change of existence for a man who has counted so much, all his life, on family spirit. Divorced from his football family at Elland Road; separated for most of the week from his own family and living in a London hotel room; spending his early evenings jogging round the circumferences of football pitches populated by Italian and Spanish waiters.

Remember too that Don Revie has always been a track-suit manager who *enjoys* taking training and the close proximity of players.

'Aren't you finding it,' I asked him, 'rather lonely?' And having put the question, it occurred to me immediately that 'lonely' was a silly adjective to toss at the man who is at the very heart of English football. 'Perhaps lonely isn't quite the right word,' I added, hastily.

'Lonely?' he said, and paused, and in Revie's rich flow

of words he does not pause often, then: 'Lonely is the right word,' he said, without sadness but with meaning.

That was a couple of weeks ago. Now it is October, and on the 30th day of this month the England team meet Czechoslovakia at Wembley, and play for the first time under Don Revie's managership. A great many people, both inside and outside the sport, are hoping that October will see the beginning of a quiet revolution in English international football.

When Don Revie was approaching the end of his playing career, at Leeds, he decided to apply for the advertised post as manager at Bournemouth. The then Chairman of Leeds, Harry Reynolds, when he heard of Revie's application, considered the man's character; his qualities and his qualifications, and announced to the Leeds United Board: 'If Don is good enough to manage Bournemouth, he's good enough to manage Leeds United.'

Now, Don Revie sets out to prove that if he was good enough to manage Leeds United, he's good enough to manage England.

20 FRIENDLY ENCOUNTER

From *Village Hall*, Granada TV, 1974

Owing to a previous mix-up, two amateur football teams who are about to play each other in a friendly match, are having to change together in the village hall instead of the usual dressing-rooms. The player–managers of both teams are in their early forties, but there the similarity ends. The home team manager, ERNEST GROVES, *is a precise office clerk in local government and also a physical fitness fanatic; the away team manager,* HORACE HAYWOOD, *is an ex-pro footballer and an altogether more carefree character. While* GROVES *is performing his pre-match loosening-up exercises,* HAYWOOD, *with a cigarette dangling at the corner of his mouth, strolls across the hall to chat to him:*

HAYWOOD *(a western movie buff)*: Howdy, stranger.

GROVES *does not reply, but glares at the cigarette in*

HAYWOOD's *mouth.*

HAYWOOD: *Muchos regrettos,* senor. (*He stubs out his cigarette and sits down besides* GROVES.) I've just been totting up your scalps – you seem to be light of a substitute. We're in the same boat ourselves.
GROVES: I'm not. I've a lad who does a butcher's round until half-past two.
HAYWOOD: Really?
GROVES: We take his strip down to the pitch and he changes in the bushes, if called upon.

HAYWOOD *nods, slowly, his thoughts on other things. His eyes wander round the hall.*

143

HAYWOOD: Have you ever had a funny feeling that you've been somewhere before?

GROVES: Often.

HAYWOOD: Yes. I got it as soon as I walked in here this afternoon.

GROVES: It's not uncommon. I understand that there's a very simple scientific psychological explanation.

HAYWOOD: You don't say?

GROVES: It's all in the mind. Certain parts of the brain react before certain other parts.

HAYWOOD *nods slowly, as though digesting this information, then:*

HAYWOOD: Great. Only I have a funny feeling that I *have* been here before. Did they used to have dances in here?

GROVES: They still do. Old Tyme, Ballroom, Discos – hops.

HAYWOOD: I'm going back some years now. Fifty-four, fifty-fivish this would be. When I was a young player. I came down from the north – 'cos I was living up there in them days – and I travelled down to play in a representative match in Manchester. We stopped over for the Saturday night, me and a big thick-set full-back called Mickey Hardisty. We got a skinful of firewater and we picked up a couple of squaws in a licensed Manchester wigwam. And we got on a bus with this pair of birds and I'll swear blind they brought us back to this dive.

GROVES: It's more than probable. There's always been a regular and reliable bus service to here from Manchester Piccadilly.

HAYWOOD: Happy days. Isn't it funny how you suddenly get confronted with your mucky murky past?

GROVES *(not interested)*: You wouldn't happen to be sitting on a pair of tie-ups, by any remote chance?

HAYWOOD *looks – and he is. He hands them to* GROVES.

HAYWOOD: Sorry, senor. I wish I could remember this

bird's name. The one that dragged me here from Manchester. A big ginger-headed lass, and did she have a pair on her? I'll tell you now how I remember it was here. Because while we were jigging round, doing a war-dance to a three-piece combo, and she was rubbing these big head-lamps up against me – she let it slip that she was in here twice a week with the Wolf Cubs.

GROVES, *who has been tying up his boots, pauses but remains silent.*

HAYWOOD: You know, the little lads with the green jerseys and the little neckerchiefs? *(He raises two fingers and gives the Wolf Cub salute.)* So, later, I've got her outside round the back where they keep the dustbins, haven't I? I says, 'By hell, lass,' I says, 'if this is how you carry on in the cubs, there'll be no stopping you when you join the Boy Scouts.!'

HAYWOOD *shakes his head, slowly, and laughs silently to himself in happy reminisce, before continuing:*

HAYWOOD: If you give me a minute I'll tell you what they called her. . . .
GROVES: Eleanor.
HAYWOOD: Hey-up, you could be right, it was one of them posh names. . . . *(Sudden foreboding.)* Did you know her?
GROVES: Do. The young woman you are talking about chances to be my lady wife.

There is a moment's stunned silence before HAYWOOD *recovers himself.*

HAYWOOD: No. Oh, no. I think you'll find this couldn't have been the same young woman.
GROVES: Don't distress yourself, I only mention the fact in order to save us both embarrassment before you continue further.
HAYWOOD: I think you'll find you're mistaken, pardner. Different female.

GROVES: Miss Eleanor Hardwick as she was then, *Missis* Eleanor Groves as she is now. Mother of two. She was a single lady in the days you speak about. It's of small consequence. I didn't take her out, seriously, until nineteen fifty-eight.

HAYWOOD *(shaking his head slowly but surely)*: I think you'll find the young lady that you mean is a different person to the bird I'm talking about.

GROVES: *Miss* Eleanor Hardwick, in the days which you're referring to, was a spinster lady in her late teens, *auburn*-haired, Baloo to the Wolf Cub pack. The facts aren't open to argument – facts are facts – I'm not *looking* for an argument.

HAYWOOD: I still say we've got a mix-up somewhere.

GROVES *(with a tight smile)*: Let's drop the subject, why don't we?

HAYWOOD *(rises, awkwardly)*: Yes. Well. By rights, I should be having a last few words with my goalkeeper about right-hand crosses to the far post.

GROVES *(nodding vigorously)*: By all means.

But although HAYWOOD *is anxious to leave, he finds it difficult to go without putting a final foot in it.*

HAYWOOD: Look – what I would like to say amigo, whoever the lady was – be it your missis or this different bird I think it was – well, I would just like you to know that I didn't get anywhere – anything – if you know what I mean.

GROVES *(another tight smile)*: Of course.

HAYWOOD: Not all the way – I didn't even *try* to go the whole hog. I had too much respect for her, you know what I mean? And that's all that I wanted to say.

HAYWOOD *clears his throat, noisily, and walks away.* GROVES *stands, frozen in his own thoughts, for several moments, and then goes pensively back to tying his boots.*

21 A MATTER OF PRIORITIES

ST ALBANS CITY 2, CLAPTON 4

Everybody I met who went, told me that the League Cup
Final in 1974 was an absolute cracker. Having watched
it on The Big Match on the following Sunday afternoon,
I was not disposed to argue the fact. I did have tickets for
the game. Not one, not two, not three, but four – excellent tip-up seats in the main stand. And those self-same
tickets are still lying on my desk, staring me in the face,
as I write these very words. In the final event, I was
unable to go.

What happened, you may well be wondering? Did I
trip over a *Dinky Thunderbird* toy on the bedroom stair
and break a leg on the morning of the game? Was I
struck down by high temperature and mysterious disease
on the day before?

Well, actually, no.

As a matter of fact, to admit to the *honest* truth, my
nerve cracked about two hours before the kick-off and
I opted instead for the Rothman's Isthmian League
bottom of the table clash between St Alban's City and
Clapton FC; I have been told that there are marked
traces of insanity running through my entire family
history.

'I am giving St Albans a blank this week,' I had said to
my wife some days before the game, triumphantly waving
the Wembley tickets in her face, 'and I shall give you a
well-earned treat by taking you to watch the ageless skills
of the incredible "Doog" and the magical Law.'

'Who are they?' she replied, and added unnecessarily
that if the choice was hers she would far prefer a good
film, followed by a hot dinner in a reputable restaurant.

147

I was forced to point out to her that she was totally without soul and that the two gentlemen in question were an object lesson to all men who, like myself, were watching their important years slip away at a horrifyingly dizzy pace.

'Do you mean that there are middle-*aged* men who run around in football shorts?'

'Never mind, never mind,' I said testily, and then changed tack: 'You will see them both next Saturday on Wembley's hallowed turf, you can be sure of that.'

'You said not long ago that if Leeds United lost a league match this season I could be sure that that would be the day when St Albans would win one.'

I strode from the room, with dignity, at that point. There are some women that you just can't argue with. I made the fool mistake of marrying one of them. It was true, all the same. I had made the forecast that she now accused me of and, what's more, I had even committed it to print. If I had been a rash sportswriter with a brown bowler hat I would have eaten it some weeks before.

In fact, although Leeds' gallant unbeaten run had ended, St Albans' City Football Club, on the day of which I write, had managed to labour on in their league for over six miserable months without notching up a single victory. For some time I had been daily expecting a phone call from either or both of the McWhirter twins, with an offer of inclusion for my football team in their *Guinness Book of Records*. And it was principally the story of St Albans' dismal record of failures that kept me from my trip to Wembley and the League Cup.

The all-important clash between St Albans and Clapton was a vital relegation match. And if you think that what happens at the bottom of the First Division of the Football League is Death or Glory stuff, then try supporting a struggling amateur side and you'll find that you need the ice-cool nerve and total dedication of a Kamikaze pilot.

Besides, if I had made the trip to Wembley for that game, support at St Albans had plummeted so low that season that I stood a good chance of halving the gate. There was, too, the added and pleasurable incentive that, at last, I stood a fair chance of watching my team nick win points. Clapton were only one place above us in the league and, as they had conceded 105 goals in thirty-two games, it seemed not entirely improbable that even the St Albans' forwards, on their own midden, were not without hope of getting behind, or going through, the Clapton defence. Well, in the event we did manage to score. Twice, in fact. But both of our goals came from the penalty spot. It seemed at the time as though God, in his infinite mercy, had realized all that I had sacrificed in not going to Wembley, and had laid on a *Penalty Prize* display of his own devising at St Albans football ground.

There were three penalties in all awarded during that match. And had the final result been declared on penalties then St Albans would have gained, by two goals to one, that elusive win they had so long been seeking. As things turned out, Clapton had the audacity to put the ball into our net on three more occasions and by more ingenious means, and we clocked up yet one more defeat, going down by four goals to two.

I had no complaints. Let it be admitted that St Albans did not play well – neither did Clapton, but St Albans were *awful*. They struggled, stumbled and scuttered about the pitch like blind mice while the Clapton players, scenting blood, pursued and harried my lot like vengeful clumsy farmers' wives. And if, at the end of those utterly forgettable ninety minutes on that sad Saturday afternoon, the tails of the St Albans players were not exactly severed, they were well and truly between their legs.

Facing up to fact at that moment, we were then eight points adrift, second from the bottom of the league, and relegation, it seemed, had become reality. The trouble is, in such a situation, the dedicated football fan refuses to acknowledge that reality exists. A mild form of insanity sets in. I was apt to wake up in the middle of the night computing illogical and impossible permutations on my finger-ends.

Supposing Clapton lost their next three games and we struck form and hit a winning streak? Supposing we had beaten Corinthian Casuals away, and then what if Casuals were to beat Clapton in the weeks to come, where would we have stood then? Supposing Kevin Keegan got the hump with Liverpool and turned up, with his boots, outside our dressing-room door on the following Saturday afternoon?

And then, I decided, to hell with all hypothesis.

The week after the League Cup Final I was due to make one of my bi-annual pilgrimages to Mecca. Twice a year, during the football season, I forgo St Albans City and make the trip up north to watch Leeds United. I go partly to recharge my batteries, partly to restore my confidence, and also to reassure myself that the old adrenalin can still course when opportunity arises. That season, looking back on the horrendous list of losing matches, I felt like an expensive car that had been left unused in a cold, damp garage – my engine needed to be run occasionally or otherwise it would have rusted up.

I owned two tickets for a forthcoming Leeds v. Burnley match at Elland Road. Two fine tip-up seats in the main stand. And those very tickets are still lingering on my desk somewhere as I write these words, they are tucked away beneath a box of paper clips.

'I'm taking you up to Leeds in a couple of weeks' time,' I remember telling my wife. 'You will see the wee wizard, Billy Bremner himself, *and* Norman Hunter, *and* Johnny Giles, *and* Allan Clarke, *and* all the rest of the lads . . .'

'You said I would be going to Wembley to see Wolves play Manchester City a couple of weeks ago,' she sighed.

It is true, I had said that.

I seem to collect unused football tickets like some people collect beer-mats. . . .

22 ILLEGAL APPROACH

From *Second House* BBC TV, 1974

A working class living-room. HARRY BULLOCK; *his wife,* LILIAN; *and their fifteen-year-old son* RORY, *are seated around the dining-table, eating cold meats and salad.* HARRY *is also studying a newspaper.*

HARRY: Hey up, the hooligans have been out in force again. Just listen to this: 'Police arrested eight youths . . .' *(He breaks off and pulls a face.)* Bloody hell-fire, aren't these pickled onions strong? 'Police arrested eight youths at the City Ground last night when violence erupted on the terraces while the teams were having a kickabout, prior to a charity friendly game.'

RORY: Who won?

HARRY: Never mind who bloody won. Eight youths arrested, just think on and take notice.

LILIAN: Well, I'm only glad your three match suspension for kicking that player is over, our Rory. At least it gets you back on the field, playing football, instead of getting into bother with the yobbos.

HARRY: He's always in bother. He can't keep out of bother. Three match suspension. I still can't understand why you found it necessary to cripple that ginger-headed full back in the first place.

RORY: Because he was kicking lumps off me right through the first half.

HARRY: He's a dirty bugger. He's always been a dirty bugger, that ginger-headed lad. Right through his entire playing career, from when he kicked off in the Junior Infants side, up until he made it in the fourteen-and-unders. But that doesn't give you the right to do him under the referee's nose, does it?

LILIAN: Your dad's right, Rory. It's only common sense. Besides, it's too obvious in this day and age, going over the ball to your opponent. You have to use more subtle tactics – wait till the referee's elsewhere engaged and *then* chin the other player.

There is a knock at the door.

HARRY: Was that our front door? Isn't it bloody marvellous? It's always at meal-times, isn't it? The minute you sit down somebody comes knocking.
LILIAN: I'll go.

LILIAN *goes out.* HARRY *looks at his paper again and 'tut-tuts'.*

HARRY: I'd put a stop to it. I'd bring the birch back, if it was up to me. I'd end the violence.

LILIAN *returns, ushering in a football scout in his late forties,* ARNOLD MACKINTOSH.

LILIAN: It's a gentleman from the United, Harry. He's come to make an approach for our Rory's services.
ARNOLD: How do you do, Mr Bullock? Now then, Rory.

ARNOLD *extends his hand but* HARRY *hides behind his newspaper.*

ARNOLD: Arnold Mackintosh. Chief scout.
HARRY: No.
ARNOLD: Pardon?
HARRY: No.
ARNOLD: 'No' what? How do you mean, Mr Bullock, 'no'?
HARRY: No, he's not coming to the United.
ARNOLD: Now, hold hard, Mr Bullock, you're jumping the gun a trifle, surely? Who said anything about Rory coming to United? As I understand the situation, he's already signed schoolboy forms with the Rovers, hasn't he?

BULLOCK: To what do we owe the bloody pleasure, then, if you're not chasing him?

ARNOLD: Purely social. Just showing my face, making it known. I have admired the lad for a couple of seasons, I readily admit that. (*To* RORY.) I saw you clatter that ginger-headed full back. My word, you did clog him, didn't you?

RORY: He'd been kicking lumps out of me all afternoon.

ARNOLD: Your handling of the situation was hardly the epitome of finesse.

LILIAN: We all make mistakes, Mr Mackintosh.

ARNOLD: Three match suspension he got, wasn't it?

LILIAN: He's a bit impulsive, bless him, our Rory. But he's a good lad at heart. We've had a talk with him, his dad and me, he'll wait, next time he clobbers anyone, until the referee's attention is directed elsewhere.

ARNOLD: He's young. He's nobbut a lad, I suppose. He'll learn.

HARRY: Well, he won't learn at United, that's for sure.

ARNOLD: He's decided to stick with the Rovers, has he, muck or nettles?

HARRY: Maybe. That remains to be seen. We've had one chap round from the City after him.

ARNOLD: Tommy Capstick, was it?

HARRY: It's not for me to say. It might have been.

ARNOLD: I'll bet it was. The crafty bastard. He didn't talk cash, I hope, did he?

HARRY: My lips are sealed. He might have done.

ARNOLD: The diabolical sod! That's an illegal approach, you know, in football parlance. If Rory's signed schoolboy forms for Rovers, it's a criminal offence for him to be offered cash by another club, it's punishable by law.

LILIAN: I thought it was funny at the time, only I didn't like to say anything.

ARNOLD: This cash, was there any specific sum mentioned, or was it left in the air?

HARRY: I'm sworn to secrecy. But I'll drop a hint. If

153

you were to hazard a guess in the region of three hundred pounds, you wouldn't be far short of the mark.

ARNOLD: It's rampant corruption! It's behaviour like that that gets football a bad name.

LILIAN: There was also reference made to a motor car, over and above the cash offer.

ARNOLD: No! There never was! What kind?

HARRY: A small two-door family job.

ARNOLD: Second-hand?

HARRY: Brand new.

ARNOLD: They've always been bent, the City lot. They want reporting to the FA.

HARRY: No final decision was made.

ARNOLD *holds up a plastic carrier bag.*

ARNOLD: You see, take my position. Purely by chance, right at this moment, I happen to be carrying five hundred quid in used oncers in here. Supposing, by mischance, I was to put this bag down here on your table and walk off without it, forgetfully, leave it behind – because of this chap Captstick's blatant disregard of sporting protocol, you mjght get the wrong impression entirely and think that I was putting in a bid for Rory on United's behalf.

LILIAN: And wouldn't you be?

ARNOLD: Never. Nothing could be further from my mind. It'd be a mental blockage. Lapse of memory. Mind you, if Rory fancied a run out with our Juniors, he'd only have to pop round to the ground any Saturday morning. With his boots, of course.

RORY: I've already signed on schoolboy forms to the Rovers though.

HARRY: He can't even turn out for them without his headmaster's permission first.

LILIAN: It's disgraceful really, isn't it? When you think about it. Fifteen years old and his life's not his own.

HARRY: When I was his age I was getting good money doing overtime on a building site.

ARNOLD: There's ways and means, Mr Bullock. To give you an example. We could always play him under an assumed name.

LILIAN: Is that allowed?

ARNOLD: It's bending the rules a teeny-weeny bit, agreed. Then again, what are the rules for, if not to be bent? (*To* RORY.) Schoolboy forms don't tie you down for ever, lad. You'll have to sign professional with a club one day.

RORY: I quite like the Rovers.

LILIAN: It's not just a question of what you *like*, Rory. You have to look at it all ends round.

ARNOLD: By bloody hell, doesn't carrying money make your arm ache?

And he carefully places the plastic carrier bag in the centre of the table.

HARRY: You see what it is, there's still the question of the motor-car.

ARNOLD: It's funny you should mention that. We were after a young lad at the start of last season. A bit like your Rory, strangely enough, he had commitments elsewhere. Do you know, his dad woke up one morning and there was this car parked right outside his front door. We never found out where it came from. Nobody never claimed it. He's driving it to this day.

HARRY: Was that a small two-door family job?

ARNOLD: More in the nature of a four-door saloon.

LILIAN: Mind you, there's still the question of our Rory's further education to be taken into account.

ARNOLD: How do you mean, Mrs Bullock, further education? I'm not quite with you?

HARRY: They have this scheme at the Rovers. If he stays with them when he leaves school, they let him go to the Polytechnic three time a week, in the afternoons.

ARNOLD: Is that a fact?

LILIAN: To fit him for his later life. And he can learn to be whatever he likes. He can learn to be a master bricklayer, or he can learn to be a book-keeper, or he can learn to be a chartered accountant, if he frames himself.

ARNOLD: Personally speaking, I'd like to see him learn to kick with his left foot as well as he does with his right.

HARRY: Hey, he does have a tendency towards that failing.

ARNOLD (*to* RORY): That ginger-headed full back. Which foot did you clog him with?

RORY: My left peg, going over the ball.

ARNOLD: Yes, I thought it must have been at the time. If you'd got him with your right, he'd still have been hospitalized.

HARRY: I've worried about his left foot, many and many a time. I've gone without sleep sometimes.

ARNOLD: We'd have him in for extra training, Mr Bullock. Every afternoon. He'd have no time at the United for the Polytechnic.

LILIAN: But what about his education?

ARNOLD: Educated footballers, Mrs Bullock, are more trouble than they are bloody worth! And I speak as one who knows.

LILIAN: What'll become of him though? When he hangs them up? He can't go on and on, playing football. He has to consider his after-life.

ARNOLD: That's up to Rory himself, Mrs Bullock, isn't it? If he behaves himself, does as he's told, goes to bed early, keeps away from the dog-tracks, lays off the pop, steers clear of the scrubbers under the main stand, looks after his money and puts a little bit away every week – you never know your luck, he could end up as the sole owner of a fish and chip shop in West Hartlepool by the time he's thirty-five.

LILIAN: The possibility of a gents' boutique had crossed our minds.

ARNOLD: I wouldn't advise it. Not all that many of them stand the test of time.

HARRY: Hey, I hope you're paying attention, Rory, it's for your own good what we're talking about.

ARNOLD: My goodness me, is it really as late as that? I'll have to fly. There's a seven-year-old midfield player we're keeping an eye on, he's playing in a representative juvenile match tonight. Now, let me see – I didn't bring anything in here with me, did I?

Carefully, with elaborate exaggeration, he lifts the carrier bag off the table, looks underneath it, and puts it down again.

ARNOLD: No, nothing at all. Only I have to be careful, I suffer from a forgetful turn of mind.

LILIAN: I'm sure it's been a great pleasure talking to you, Mr Mackintosh, and could you leave me and my hubby two tickets for your directors' box at the main gate for next Saturday's cup clash, if it's no great inconvenience?

ARNOLD: I shall be delighted to oblige. Don't bother to see me out.

HARRY: Hey, Ignorant, say good night to Mr Mackintosh.

RORY: G'night, Mr Mackintosh.

ARNOLD: G'night, lad. And don't forget, any Saturday morning, down the ground, with your boots. Don't get up, anybody.

Nobody has shown any intention of getting up. MACKIN-TOSH *goes out. A pause. The* BULLOCKS *go back to their meal.*

LILIAN: Now, that's what I *call* a gentleman.

HARRY: Definitely one of nature's own.

LILIAN: And he talked a lot of sense. He knows his football.

HARRY: Brilliant. But I'll tell you what, we ought to play safe and hang on and see if City want to up his offer though.

HARRY *picks up the carrier-bag, takes out a handful of notes and counts them, under his breath.*

RORY: Do you want to know something? I don't mind it

at the Rovers. I was quite looking forward to going to the Polytechnic, in many ways.

HARRY: Don't you be so bloody cheeky!

LILIAN: And take your elbows off the table, I don't know where you get it from, my lad. I'll learn you to do as you're told.

Silence. HARRY *goes back to counting the one pound notes. He looks up and frowns.*

HARRY: Bugger me, these pickled onions aren't half strong! They're giving me gyp at the back of my throat!

The meal continues.

23 BIGMAL AND BILLY-GOAT CLUFF

A Grimm Moral with a Fairy-tale

From the *Evening Standard*, 1974

Once upon a time, in a far-off land, there dwelt a noble-man who discovered a liquid that was said to possess rare and magical powers. The nobleman called his liquid champagne. Rich merchants sailed their ships to the four corners of the world where they sold the magic drink, and prospered.

But the merchants sold the champagne in one land where the people were but lowly folk, toss-pots and beer-swillers for the most part, who had never heard of the liquid and knew not to what purpose it might be put.

'Throw it away,' said some, 'for surely it contains great evil!'

'Nay,' cried others. 'Destroy it not, for it is possessed of strong magic!'

Then the wise men of the land were summoned, and they studied the curious bottles and held long council.

'This is what we have decided,' said the wise men of that land. 'The liquid was brought from across the sea, and to the sea must it be returned. Therefore shall you anoint your new boats before they first set sail, and the magic liquid shall see to it that your boats return safely from their voyaging.'

As the wise men had decreed, so it was done. The bottles of champagne were broken over the prows of the boats, and though the boats went out into rough waters they never failed to return to harbour.

Now, in that country there were roving bands of men that did join weekly in battle, one with another, and these bands were called Footerclubs.

'Let us also have this magic liquid,' clamoured the

Footerclub warriors. 'For if it brings good fortune to the boats, may it not bring luck to mankind also?'

Thus it came to pass that the men of the Footerclubs took the champagne and used it as it was used on the boats, anointing themselves and pouring it over their heads. And each time two Footerclubs had been joined in great battle, the victorious ones anointed themselves afterwards and grinned, toothlessly, as they bathed together, washing away the grime and gore of combat.

And such became the custom of that country.

But there was one Footerclub that had not been victorious on the field of battle, therefore the men of that club had not been anointed.

'How can this be?' cried their leader, who was named Bigmal. 'Why should we not share in the magic liquid?'

But his men were afraid, and drew back, for such was not the custom of that land.

Thus did Bigmal summon the scribes of the country together, saying unto them: 'I am Bigmal. I am powerful. I too have the magic lotion.'

And as he spoke, he anointed himself. And because he was a man who spoke much, some of the liquid ran into his mouth. The scribes watched, anxiously, for never before in that land had anyone been known to drink the stuff.

'Is it good?' asked the scribes.

'It is very good,' answered Bigmal.

Then Bigmal made it his practice to pour the liquid down his throat each week, in front of the scribes, even though his Footerclub continued to suffer.'

'Is it good?' asked the scribes.

'It is very good,' said Bigmal.

Now, Bigmal had an ally whose name was Cluff, for they were both in the self-same leaky boat, and they preached often together to the people. And Cluff followed in the ways of Bigmal and he too drank the magic liquid.

In this way did Bigmal and Cluff try to fashion custom.

But all the other Footerclubs remained steadfast and faithful to the old ways – these were clubs led by men called Revie and Shankly and Adamson (thus named because he was the son of Adam), and Mackay from the North, and these men only used the magic liquid to anoint their warriors, and only after they had been victorious in battle.

Thus the clubs of Revie and Shankly and Adamson (son of Adam) and Mackay from the North, prospered. But the clubs of Cluff and Bigmal laboured.

MORAL: *A bottle of warm non-vintage bubbly in the players' bath is worth a case of chilled Dom Perignom in the manager's office.*

NEXT WEEK: How The Enchanted Big Cigar Failed To Light Up Crystal Palace.

24 GIANT-KILLING

The dust it seems has hardly settled from the First Round of the FA Cup – the self-same dust that was bitten in the 1973–4 season by Brighton and Hove, and Newport County and Crewe Alexandra – before the Second Round is upon us and they're steaming out and at it again, the so-called giant-killers in search of greater glories.

But on one particular chill day in late autumn, while the last of the tadpoles and minnows thrashed haplessly around in the FA Cup pool, playing their own particular brands of non-league kick-and-scuttle, and joined in combat with the remaining relatively monolithic giants of the Third and Fourth Divisions, I was wistfully moping on a lonely terrace in amateur football, watching St Albans City play out a humble league fixture.

The point I wish to make is that if you are under the impression that the struggle for the most-prized trophy in English football gets under way towards December – you couldn't be more wrong. For the vast majority of the competition's participants, it has been long since over and done with. For although it is officially labelled the 'Third Round' when the First and Second Division League clubs take an interest, it is in fact the *umpteenth* round for all the aspiring amateurs.

And if you think that the Qualifying and Preliminary rounds of the FA Cup are unimportant – then you've never given your whole heart to a team with a name like Ellesmere Port Town, or Stocksbridge Works Social, or Billingham Synthonia, or Irthlingborough Diamonds, or how about Connah's Quay Nomads? To say nothing of

those perennial cup campaigners, Blaenau Ffestiniog.
And only those supporters who have shivered behind the
goalposts at a Qualifying Round and shouted *'Come on
Blaenau Ffestiniog!'* for a full ninety minutes, will know
the reason why they find it difficult to make the First
Round Proper.

My own St Albans City stalwarts renounced the Cup
competition quite early in the season – they took hardly
a step down soccer's Appian Way before faltering and
falling out, swamped by five goals to nil, by Dartford in
the First Round Qualifying.

In those slap-happy starter days of the competition,
Dartford, the Leeds United of the Southern League, was
a Goliath to be feared in the draw. But as round follows
round, and the big boys stick their oars in, the Goliaths
become the Davids, and in the hurly-burly of soccer it is
the Davids that often take a tumble. Somewhere along
the way, Dartford went too in 1974.

Soccer analysts, shock-happy football-writers and
hysterical TV commentators will tell you that *'Giant-
killing is what the FA Cup is all about.'*

Don't believe a word of it.

The sad truth about giant-killing and the Cup is that

there are far too many giant-killers chasing far too few giants. For of the 292 non-league clubs that started out in the 1973–4 competition, only twelve did battle in the Second Round Proper. And the real giants, the lads from the First and Second Divisions don't even lace their boots up for that one.

No, most of the giant-killing deeds in football are firmly rooted, where they belong, in the realms of pipe-and-day-dreams, like they are in the fairy stories.

Happily, there are odd exceptions.

Whenever football talk gets around to tales of amateur derring-do and of giant-killers in actual performance, then the feat of Isthmian Leaguers, Walthamstow Avenue, is fondly recalled. For it was Walthamstow, you may remember, who went up to Old Trafford and held the might of Manchester United to a goalless draw, having struggled through to the Fourth Round Proper, way back in 1952–3. And that was arguably the best performance ever by an amateur side. Even so, can it really count as giant-*killing*? Hardly, for the giant got up off the floor and won the replay, at Highbury, by 4 goals to 2.

And how far back must we go through the record books to discover the last time that an amateur side knocked out a First or Second Division club? Frankly, I don't know. Perhaps your record books go back further than mine?

Supporters of semi-pro football, of course, have not to look back far into history to find their boost to confidence. For it was only a couple of short seasons ago that Hereford, then in the Southern League, sent Newcastle United spinning from the competition. A result that no doubt helped inspire their rapid progress, having won election to the Football League, to their present respectable position in the Third Division.

As for the hopes, dreams and ambitions of all the semi-pros and amateurs that get through as far as the Second Round of the FA Cup in any season: *Nil Desperandum*, lads, say I.

For some of them *must* get through each year to square up to their own particular giants – if only by the simple artifice of knocking out each other.

Then, on a Saturday night in every season, after the Second Round is over, a number of exhausted, bruised, battered but supremely happy amateur and part-time footballers drift up to their beds and dream of running on to the pitch at White Hart Lane or Stamford Bridge or even Anfield. And the lucky non-league committee men dream their dreams too of First Division opposition – dreams of spectators in their thousands clicking through the turnstiles. Because *money* is what the F A Cup is *really* all about to the impecunious members of the F A family.

And I have my dreams too – impossible dreams of Cup results such as: Arsenal 0, Stocksbridge Works Social 1; or Tottenham Hotspur 1, Irthlingborough Diamonds 2. Or how about an F A Cup Final with a result which reads: Leeds United 3, Blaenau Ffestiniog 4. Now that really *would* be giant-killing!

25 A LOAD OF OLD ANALYSIS

For some extraordinary and, to me at least, totally inexplicable reason, not a single sports editor invited me to represent him in the press-box at Frankfurt's football stadium for Scotland's crunch match with Yugoslavia, in June, 1974. I decided, therefore, that if I couldn't be at the actual game, I would do the next best thing and watch it in surroundings where the tension would be rare, the conversation informed and intelligent, and the company impeccable. In short, I chose to spend that particular afternoon in a TV studio with a bunch of TV's soccer panellists.

ITV or BBC, I had asked myself. And after much thought, I settled for joining Brian Moore and his bunch of trendies, rather than sitting in with Jimmy Hill and his more sober-suited chappies. The final decision was made, I might add, not because I fancied the sartorial elegance of the commercial lot's tartan jackets, but rather because I shuddered at the thought of getting within the firing line of a bad joke from Lawrie McMenemy.

Having made my choice, a quick phone call and the matter was settled. I have friends in high places. The Head of Sport for London Weekend Television said that he would be delighted to have me in his studio, provided I behaved myself, remained shtum, and kept well out of the way of his perambulating cameras – which is why you didn't spot me on the telly, rubbing shoulders with the mighty.

All the same, I enjoyed myself immensely.

To refresh your memory, the soccer experts I met up

with on the ITV panel, tartan jackets and all, were those engaging highland laddies: Bobby Moncur, Paddy Crerand, Derek McDougan, Malcolm McAllison, and Big Brian (Jock) Moore. Your actual Laird of London Weekend himself, Brian McCloughie, had been given the day off and was reported to be at his wee hoose the noo' in McBrighton, munching a haggis butty.

I spent the first part of the afternoon in idyllic surroundings, watching two race meetings at once on a battery of television screens in the World Cup Office. Not only that, but I also had the good sense to put my money on Caius, a 5–2 winner, and Assett, which romped home at 5–1 – the shrewdness of my racing judgement being unimpaired by the fact that Paddy Crerand was singing: 'Six foot two, eyes of blue, Big Jim Holton's after you . . .' in the background.

'Do you often back winners?' asked a puzzled sports producer, as though mentally earmarking me for a post as a new TV tipster. 'Not often, no,' I admitted truthfully. The sports producer sighed, went about his sports producing business, and John Rickman lived to tip another day.

All the same, by three o'clock, which was the time we were due to go down to the World Cup studio, I was £13·50 in front, having also picked up place money on a well-priced outsider.

The panel, meanwhile, had gone through a sort of preliminary rough-and-ready rehearsal, more for the benefit of the studio technicians, it seemed, than to give the lads a chance to sharpen up their epigrams and witticisms. As I took my seat, a tasty make-up lady was dabbing powder at Brian Moore's receding hairline.

'Fifteen seconds, studio!' boomed a disembodied voice. And then we were transmitting. Dutifully, as ordered, I remained totally shtum and hid myself away from the prowling TV cameras.

I was not the only interloper in the studio. Clydesider,

Jim Reid, was down in London and had free-loaded in on Paddy Crerand's invitation.

The panel's pre-match chat on Scotland's chances that afternoon was informed, albeit cautious.

'They *might* do it,' said Malcolm Allison.

'They're in with a *chance*,' opined Bobby Moncur.

'It could be a *draw*,' mused Derek Dougan.

'I fancy them a *little* bit,' observed Paddy Crerand, thoughtfully.

At Brian Moore's prompting they expanded further, still slightly dubious, as to *how* they thought that Scotland might snatch at opportunities. It was Allison's opinion that the Scots might catch the Yugoslavs ball-watching. Dougan said that the Yugoslavs were open to be exploited from corners. Crerand reckoned that Bremner and his lads could achieve the impossible by concentrating their attack on the left-hand side of the Yugoslav defence. The mood was changing from one of doubt to that of cautious optimism.

There was talk too, at length, of how it was neither good nor right nor fair to players to uproot them from their wives and families and lock them away in a hotel for four weeks. Which was strange, coming from a panel of men who had themselves been uprooted from their wives and families and settled in a hotel near the studio for the duration of the competition. Particularly as one of them had told me not half an hour before, that he was 'having the time of his life, breakfast in bed, watching football all day long and getting paid for it.'

Pause for commercial break, after which we were no longer transmitting from the studio, but receiving pictures and commentary direct from Frankfurt.

We all relaxed.

'Can somebody get Jimmy Reid a cup of tea?' asked Paddy Crerand, solicitously. Two studio men, both obviously fully paid-up Union men, rushed to oblige.

'Right, lads, jackets off,' said Brian Moore. And off came all the tartan coats and even Jimmy Reid rolled his sleeves up. I settled myself happily in my chair and prepared to drink in the informed comments and intelligent analysis that lay in store for me from the mouths of my professional footballing companions.

On the screen, almost immediately after the kick-off, a Scottish pass went dangerously astray.

'Oh shit,' said Derek Dougan, thus setting the level of comment for the afternoon.

'Go *on*, Sandy, go *on*, Sandy!' screamed Paddy Crerand.

'Get into him, Jim! *Kill* him, Jim!' exhorted someone of Jim Holton.

'Far post – it's a far post ball!' from Malcolm Allison.

'Oh, come *on*, Billy, oh, come *on*, Billy!' groaned Paddy Crerand, who is blessed with the gift of poetic repetition.

'Diabolical that! Di-a-bloody-bolical!' and 'Penalty, you bugger!' someone shouted at the game's arbiter.

'Who is this bloody referee?' asked someone else.

'He's a Mexican,' said Brian Moore.

'He's a bloody Mexican bandit,' said another.

''E's a quick bugger, int 'e, Oblak?' observed Malcolm Allison, thoughtfully.

'Oh shit,' said Derek Dougan, as danger again threatened. Paddy Crerand, in his excitement, was bobbing up and down like a schoolboy impatient for the lavatory.

The first half of the game sped away like nobody's business. The dialogue in the studio may not have been informed, it may not have been intelligent, but it had been enthralling and totally engrossing.

'Jackets on, lads,' said Brian Moore, about a minute before the end of the first half. The panellists donned their tartan coats and the make-up lady rushed forward to dab again at Brian Moore's shining and perspiring forehead. 'As soon as we've taken the commercial break,' he said, 'I'll come to you again for quick one-line reactions.'

Which seemed odd, because I thought he'd been hearing quick one-line reactions for forty-five minutes.

Fag-ends, cigar-butts, plastic tea-cups, a Clydeside Union man and a buckshee *Evening Standard* sports-writer all disappeared like magic – the studio was back on transmission during the game's interval.

'So far so good,' murmured Brian Moore to the nation, and then invited his colleagues' comments. I held my breath and waited for the common language of the terraces to hit the ether.

'What a performance,' said Derek Dougan, soberly.

'They're sure to win,' murmured a suave Malcolm Allison, of Scotland's chances.

'The Yugoslavs must be a little worried,' was the urbane opinion of a collected Paddy Crerand.

'Scotland are the best side,' analysed a cool, calm Bobby Moncur. 'They're sure to win if they keep pegging away without getting too excited.'

Without getting too excited? Precisely. All they had to do, it seemed, was behave exactly as the lads in the studio were doing. And as soon as the second half was under way and the studio microphones were once more out of action, the analysts were at it again.

'Oh shit,' said Derek Dougan, getting the ball immediately rolling. He repeated those exact words twice more during the second half: once when the news was flashed on the monitor that Brazil were leading Zaïre by three goals to nil, and again when the Yugoslavs struck with their goal. Dougan's phrase, at that precise moment in time, seemed charged with majestic eloquence.

The panel's comments when the final whistle came were entirely unprintable. Their subsequent remarks to the cameras, when we were once again transmitting, were masterly understatements.

'What a shame,' said Brian Moore.

'I'm disappointed. I'm very disappointed,' said Paddy Crerand, his face as crumpled as last week's bed-linen.

Outside the studio, in the corridor, I met an elated producer. 'You won't *believe* the shot we got of Paddy's face when the Yugoslavs scored,' he said. 'Tragic. A tragic-shattered Scots supporter.' I told him that I did believe him.

I also told him that, despite the result, I had enjoyed my afternoon immensely, and could I come back and do it again sometime, perhaps on the afternoon of the World Cup Final? He said probably, but it would depend upon the content of the article I wrote about his programme. Well, this was it. He also entertained me in his Hospitality Room, hospitably, at the end of the afternoon's transmission. It was then that my own reaction to the dismal result set in, and I went on drinking.

It was after one o'clock in the morning when I poured Jim Reid into a taxi. He was going, for some reason that still eludes me, to East Sheen. He had been a Scottish supporter alone in London on Scotland's night of tragedy, and I had taken him out and wined him and dined him. At least I had done something. It did not occur to me, until much later, that Jim and I had spent about six hours in each other's company on that sad Saturday night, we had argued and we had chatted, but not once – never, in the whole course of the evening – did we mention football.

26 HUMBLE FARE

From the *Evening Standard*, 1974

I was one of the few men in England who was not surprised at the extravagant wheelings and dealings, engi-
neered by wealthy chairman Keith Cheeseman at Dunstable Town Football Club, at the start of the 1974–75
season. The offer to Sir Alf Ramsey, the signing of Jeff
Astle, the breathlessly awaited entrance of George Best
into the sporting arena – all of these, at the time, left me
completely cold. For, in fact, I had held Dunstable Town
F C in some awe ever since the beginning of the previous
season. Since the day when I was served with a potato
crisp sandwich in the shoe-box-sized refreshment room
at the Southern League Club.

In those far-off days, Barry Fry, now manager of
Dunstable Town, was playing for St Albans City. St
Albans were playing a pre-season friendly with Dunstable
and, in my role of St Albans supporter, I was alone and
palely loitering on the empty Dunstable terraces. At
half-time, as God is my witness, I was served with a
potato crisp sandwich.

For the benefit of non-gourmets, perhaps I should
explain that a potato crisp sandwich is just that: two
medium slices of thinly margarined bread supplied with
a sparse filling of potato crisps.

At first, I thought that I was the unintended victim
of some foolish footballing practical joke. Footballers, if
I am to believe the popular Sunday press, are lovable
practical jokers to a man. The potato crisp sandwich I
was in possession of – indeed, had *paid* for – was obviously
the handiwork of a dull-witted but fun-loving full back,
and was a prank intended to be foisted on to his buffoonish

striker chum. I took the wretched article back to the counter immediately after I had bitten into it.

'Excuse me,' I said to the man behind the tea-urn, 'but this sandwich has got potato crisps in it.'

'Yes,' he said curtly, 'it's a potato crisp sandwich.'

Too stunned to reply, I walked away. When I had recovered myself sufficiently, I offered my potato crisp sandwich to a stray mongrel dog that was cocking an exploratory leg up against the wall of the committee room, but the cur sniffed and loped off.

Well, in France the natives nibble at the haunches of frogs; in the Rain Forests of New Guinea, or so I am led to believe, the pigmies consider that small white grubs dug out from beneath the bark of rotting trees are a rare delicacy – at Dunstable Town Football Club, a potato crisp sandwich is looked upon as ideal fare for a football fan.

To each his own.

But now that Mr Cheeseman and his equally well-heeled comrade, Mr Bill Parrish, had joined the club, potato crisp sandwiches and Dunstable Town F C were surely poles apart? Or were they?

After all, nobody had fully explained the full story behind a £700 bill that Mr Cheeseman was reputed to have coughed up for in a London night club. You can get an awfully woozy lot of champers for 700 quid. Was it possible that those worthy gentlemen of Dunstable had dined off something extraordinary on that extravagant evening?

'Waiter?'

'Yes, zair?'

'Me and my chums would like to order something I can't seem to find on your menu?'

'Ze compliments of the managair, zair – your wish is his command.'

'Rightyho, then, ask the chef to take a glass of director's port with me, and inquire if he can knock up a plateful of potato crisp sandwiches?'

'Excuse me, zair, did you say crisp sandwiches?'

'You heard, Alfonso – chop-chop, double-quick.'

Collapse of small Italian waiter who, after being revived with a few splashes of iced-water from a Dom Perignom ice-bucket, scuttles away to the kitchen, and returns:

'Excuse me, zair. Ze chef would like to know what flavour of ze crisps you would prefair – ze roast chicken or ze smokey bacon?'

'Oh, make 'em plain – I never could stand spicy foreign muck.'

'Very good, zair. But I am afraid they will be – 'ow you say? – expensive.'

''Ow much?'

'A hundred pounds each.'

'Done. We'll have seven!'

It had also been reported that, on the same night of merry-making, those members of the Dunstable jet-set chartered a flight in order to continue their celebrations in the north of England. Now why, in the name of Slack Alice, should any man in his right mind go gadding off to Manchester in the middle of the night to seek out pleasure? Unless there is an epicurean brand of potato crisp sandwich, perhaps, to be had only in the magical city where the moon shines brightly out of every puddle? Up there, of course, they are known colloquially as tatie crisp butties, and they give the taste buds an extra tang when you bite into the small blue bag of salt that is carefully hidden in every sandwich.

Another thought occurred. Barry Fry was reported as saying that George Best would travel down on match-days 'by chauffeur-driven Lamborghini or Mercedes.' One wondered, as whichever sleek luxury vehicle it was that cruised down each Saturday morning, and its passenger surveyed the passing scene, looking for recommended luncheon hostelries where the peppered *filet* steaks where flared to a nicety – or the waitresses had got big knockers – would the chauffeur manage to fob off George's demands for a request stop?

'No need to pull up for luncheon, Mr Best, sir. The chairman has provided a packed lunch in the boot – there are several of Dunstable's best potato crisp sandwiches and a bottle of vintage Tizer.'

And thus had got him to the ground on time?

But when the joking was over, and one paused to consider what had happened to the still young superstar of yesterday, I brought back to memory Derek Dougan's comment, made on ITV's World Cup panel just prior to the West Germany–Holland game. When asked if Cruyff was the greatest footballer in the world, the Doog replied 'Johann Cruyff is brilliant and was made on earth; but Georgie Best was made in heaven.'

And, agreeing with Dougan's words, I could only feel an infinite sadness that a man of Best's genius, with his capacity for entertaining and delighting millions with his sheer uncomplicated artistry, should in that come-back attempt resort to a brand of dismal football played out in slovenly grounds, in front of empty terraces, and where hopes and dreams would seem to be fashioned from such stuff as potato crisp sandwiches are made of.

Is there something wrong with George, one wonders, or is there something wrong with football?

DUNSTABLE TOWN 4, GLOUCESTER CITY I

Having not been back to Dunstable Town Football Club since the day I was served a potato crisp sandwich in the shoe-box tea-room, I was a little unsure of the route.

My taxi-driver was even less informed than myself, having never before made the journey to the club in his life. 'Keep an eye out for the floodlights,' I suggested as we entered the outskirts of the town and cruised past the College Christmas Cracker Company Limited.

I should have known better. Dunstable Town Football Club doesn't run to floodlights. Only a couple of weeks before, in fact, a Football League manager had told me a sorry tale about how he had once made the trip down from the North to the Southern League outfit in order to watch a player in a midweek fixture and had turned up at the ground ten minutes before the final whistle.

Because of the club's shortcomings in the matter of floodlighting equipment, the evening kick-off had taken place at 6.15 instead of 7.30. My manager friend had made an unnecessary journey down the M1.

'How can a club that can't afford floodlights afford Georgie Best?' he had asked me, with understandable bewilderment.

And at the time, I could only shake my head, shrug my shoulders and share his puzzlement.

Of course, now that the silly pre-season is over and the season-proper under way, we all know the truth – Dunstable CAN'T afford Mr Best's regular services. Even if they could, it has now become apparent that the tubby but still talented little fellow has not the slightest intention of putting his name at the bottom of any club's contract.

George, it transpires, sees himself as a one-man world-wide travelling road-show, picking up the kudos by flitting from club to club, turning out in all kinds of boring exhibition matches and lifeless friendlies, but never ever getting involved in the real nitty-gritty of competitive sport. It sounds to me like the living death of football, but if that is what he really wants, then I wish him well.

But what has happened to the club where George's shadow fluttered for a fleeting instant? And isn't it curious to realize that, for all his meanderings, George Best has only worn the colours of two football clubs in this country: Manchester United and Dunstable Town?

All of which is why I made the journey over to Dunstable last Saturday afternoon, to see how the side was faring now that its wayward Superstar has done another moody. And to discover how many of the local thousands who had packed the ground to watch George turn it on against Manchester United Reserves, had decided to stick with the club without Best, for better or for worse.

Not very many, I'm sad to say. Dunstable Town's League fixture last Saturday was with Gloucester City. The kick-off was scheduled for 3 p.m. and at 2.45 when I arrived at the ground, the crowd could be counted on the fingers of both hands.

Half a dozen small boys were wrestling on the turf in front of the trainer's bench; a lady in a pink frock was selling raffle tickets (five for 10p) for non-League footballs obligatory prize of a cardboard box containing fruit: and there was a thoughtful man with a large brass badge in his lapel that designated him the Gloucester City teams coach-driver and another man wearing a brown suit, boots and a red-and-white knitted Gloucester City supporter's hat.

All in all, it seemed a far, far cry from the packed ground, the music, the leggy majorettes and all the attendant showbiz razamatazz that had heralded Georgie Best's appearance on the Dunstable turf.

Dunstable Town Football Club, when empty, is not the prettiest of grounds. It sits snugly in the heart of a factory complex close by a motor-car break-up yard.

The man in the brown suit, boots and the knitted cap shuffled across to join me on the terrace underneath the economy-size main stand. At first, I thought his intention was that if the two of us stood close enough together we might look like the beginnings of a crowd.

I was wrong. He glowered at me, accusingly, 'I thought you were supposed to have had this bloody pitch flattened out?' he said.

'Not me personally,' I hedged, for I had got the impression that he thought I was someone else.

'You're supposed to have bloody done,' he repeated stoutly. To this day, I don't know whether he mistook me for the Dunstable chairman or the groundsman.

I drifted away from my sole companion of the terraces and moved across towards the home team's dressing-room window, which was wide open and from whence came a strong whiff of linament and the sound of raised voices.

As there were but ten minutes to go to the kick-off, I expected to hear, I suppose, the argumentative but eager and interesting talk of match tactics: how would they scheme up front, for instance, without the skills of the bright-eyed Northern Ireland boyo to baffle, beat and ping balls past the Gloucester defence?

Instead, the noisy argument that was coming out of the Dunstable dressing-room window was not about that afternoon's encounter but the forthcoming Tuesday night fixture with Corby Town. And the Dunstable players were not discussing tactics for THAT game, but quarrelling among themselves about where Corby actually was.

'It's in bloody Warwickshire,' said one player. 'It's bloody not,' said another. 'It bloody is.'

I took myself up into the stand. I can stop at home and hear THAT kind of argument.

When the match kicked-off there were twenty-four souls in all in the main stand. A figure which can be broken down as follows: ten non-paying VIPs in the fibre-board partitioned directors' box, three club officials issuing tickets and collecting loot; myself; two toddlers who were playing at running up and down the empty rows of seats; a man with a notebook who I took to be a local Press man; and six persons who had actually handed over money to sit in the stand.

And, at a quick guess, I hazarded there must have been about 100 other members of the paying public dotted around the ground. Which was a pity, because I for one quite enjoyed the football that was played. But then, I am known as one of that peculiar breed of men who like the semi-pro and amateur game.

Why? Well, for one thing, small-time football grounds still remain a good place to take the wife and kids on a warm Saturday afternoon. Admittedly, because of the lack of crowd, you can hear all the foul language that comes up off the pitch – but there's always room for the kids to run around in safety to their heart's content.

Also, the brand of football played is interesting. Take last Saturday's game, for instance. A lot of players in red shirts kept giving the ball to the players in blue shirts, who presumably in return for kindnesses received, kept giving the ball back to players in red. And that goes to provide a less skilful but more OPEN kind of football than you get at League grounds.

Again, Dunstable might not have got George Best, but they do have Jeff Astle on their books. Astle, surrounded as he was by semi-pros and amateurs, LOOKED like a proper footballer and there were precious moments during the afternoon when he showed flashes of his old brilliance that overshadowed everything else that was going on.

Astle slotted home one copybook goal, laid off the pass that made another, was instrumental in the making of a

third, and was never less than workmanlike and professional in Dunstable's 4–1 win over Gloucester.

It may even be possible that Jeff Astle finally laid the
ghost of George Best last Saturday afternoon at Creasey
Park. Certainly, there is no sign now that Best was ever
at the club. None?

Well, at half-time, outside the tea-room, I noticed a
parked, gleaming white Mercedes – presumably the self-
same one that ferried George up and down the M1.
There was no sign though of the much-mentioned
liveried chauffeur, and he for one is no doubt grateful
that his onerous driving stint to Manchester and back,
twice every Saturday is over and done.

And inside the tea-room, already peeling off a cupboard
door, there is a newspaper photograph of manager Barry
Fry, chairman Keith Cheeseman, and George Best,
standing together on the Dunstable pitch. Underneath
the photograph, there is another cutting from a local
paper that contains a reader's letter.

The letter is headed 'Thanks for the Memory' and it
takes the form of a eulogy to George Best and his brief
sojourn with the club, written by a Dunstable supporter.

But at the end of the season, Dunstable Town may
have cause to consider that League Tables are not
fashioned out of memories, however golden. They are
hewn from actual and indisputable results.

If Dunstable Town Football Club can learn that lesson
without too much heartache it will probably be Jeff Astle
that they have to thank, and not George Best.

28 AWAY FROM IT ALL

I remember, I remember. . . .

I am eight years old. I am wearing a navy-blue swimming cozzie and I am batting for Yorkshire on golden sands that are hot beneath the soles of my bare feet. The bat and tennis-ball have been carefully selected from off a Woolworth's counter; the stumps consist of a precariously balanced carrier bag and a couple of woolly jumpers. I seem to have been at the crease all afternoon, I am seeing the ball well, smacking boundaries off the back foot in all directions: sometimes as far as a fat man in a deck-chair with a Woodbine packet on his nose, sometimes as far as the edge of the sea. Australia is represented by dad, bowling medium-pace under-armers, and mum who is long-stop. I seem to remember too that there is a yapping wire-haired terrier fielding in the

deep – or is memory playing me false again and I am getting
mixed up with the dog that fielded for Lord Snooty and his
gang in The Dandy, *or was it* The Beano. . .?

We decided to take the kids off to Blackpool for Whit-
suntide this year. In doing so, I wasn't only fulfilling a
long-felt need to re-live the good life of my early childhood, I was also going to introduce my two lads to the
joys of the English seaside holiday. Beach-cricket and
beach-football, that's what seaside holidays are all about;
not watching shiftless foreign beach-boys bashing balls
with biff-bats on foreign beaches.

'Where's your cricket bat?' I say to my seven-year-old,
and I glance up from trying to squeeze two quarts of
luggage into a pint-sized suitcase.

'What cricket bat?'

'*Your* cricket bat. You know very well what cricket
bat. Don't prevaricate. The cricket bat I bought you for
your last birthday. I'm asking you where it is?'

He scratches his head, opens his mouth, hangs out his
tongue – an irritating habit he has picked up somewhere
over the past few months. I am trying to break him of it.
'I got a *Walt Disney Cassette Movie Viewer* for my last
birthday,' he says, eventually.

'You also got a very expensive cricket bat,' I tell him,
slowly, breathing hard, 'with matching stumps. Where
is it? What's happened to it?'

'Oh, *that* cricket bat,' he says it as if the house was
rotten with cricket bats. 'It got broke.'

'Broke? *Broke*! What do you mean, 'it got broke'? It
can't have got broke. Cricket bats don't *get* broke, some
body breaks them. It can't possibly have got broke. You
haven't played with that bat since the day it came into
this house.'

'It didn't get broke playing cricket. It got broke
knocking tent pegs in. In the garden.'

At which point I decide to drop the subject and to buy
a new bat once we arrive in Blackpool. After all, I was
planning to go on holiday and there seemed little sense

in giving myself apoplexy before I'd even got as far as the front gate. I continued to pack in silence and it was the boy who spoke at last.

'Can I take my *Walt Disney Cassette Movie Viewer* to Blackpool?'

'Certainly not.'

'*Why* not?'

'Because I say so. Because we are packing necessities – not toys.'

'You were going to pack the cricket bat, if it hadn't have got broke.'

'A cricket bat,' I explain, carefully keeping my voice down, 'is a piece of sporting equipment, it is not a toy.'

'Oh.' He didn't sound all that interested. After a pause, he said: 'Can we take the bagatelle board?'

End of conversation.

I remember, I remember. . . .

I am nine years old. I am wearing a pair of grey shorts and a green wolf-cub jersey and I am playing centre forward for Leeds United on golden sands that are hot beneath the soles of my bare feet. I am the proud possessor of an inflatable beach ball that has travelled with me, annually, to every seaside resort in the North of England, or so it seems. The ball is made of rubber, has alternate blue and green panels, and is dotted with bicycle-tyre repair patches – for I have owned it throughout my entire childhood. I am dribbling down the right wing, going round the Gunners' defence. Arsenal consists of my father, who wears braces over an open-necked shirt, and my mother, who is wearing a rose-pink cardigan over a flowered frock and is playing in goal. The blown-up beach ball clings to my bare instep as if it was fastened there with glue. I sidestep and dummy past dad and sprint for goal. I seem to remember, hazily, that the beach-ball once got carried out to sea and that my father was almost drowned in his efforts to rescue it – or is Old Man Memory confusing me again and did that happen to Desperate Dan when an enormous balloon towed him out to Iceland in The Beano, *or was it* The Dandy. . .?

'Where's the football?'

'Which football?' And this time it is my wife who answers.

'*My* football,' I say.

As it is with cricket bats at our house, so it is with footballs – we are not inundated with the blessed things. But I do happen to own an *Adidas* match-ball. It is mine. It belongs to me. For some reason, it was given to me by Jimmy Hill to celebrate my forty-fourth birthday. It arrived on its own, by taxi, at 8.30 a.m. on that very anniversary of my birth. I have never found out why. We have tried to give it a good home. But I am now forty-five and, to this day, the ball has never been kicked in anger. It has always seemed too good, somehow, to just take outside and punt about the lawn. It is beginning to look sad and to sag in places. Ah well, we are none of us getting any younger.

'You aren't thinking, I hope,' says my good lady, 'of taking that football to Blackpool?'

'Of course I am. What else?'

'There isn't room for it.'

'We'll *make* room.'

'What for?'

'I intend to teach the lads to play football on the sands.'

'With a *real* football?'

'Certainly,' I reply, and continue, with the wit fairly bubbling out of me: 'I have no intention of travelling with an *unreal* one.'

'People don't play on the sands with real footballs,' she informs me. 'You'll injure somebody. They use plastic footballs on the beach.'

Ah but they do not! They use rubber beach-balls that have alternate blue and green panels and are dotted with bicycle-tyre repair patches. They dribble for countless hour after hour, through the loose soft sand near the promenade, racing across the hard wet stuff closer to edge of the sea, until it seems as if the ball is attached to their instep and, in their boyhood imagination, they are the heroes of the Victoria ground or Deepdale or Elland Road or, indeed, wherever fancy lies. Thus it was when Stanley Matthews was a lad and Tom Finney and me.

In the event, I didn't take my match-ball to Blackpool. And, on arrival, I found to my disgust that I couldn't buy a rubber beach-ball with alternate blue and green panels anywhere, much as I tried. I was forced to settle, in the end, for a hideous red and orange inflatable plastic job which, when blown up, looked rather like a damp balloon. It behaved like one too, for every time it was kicked it shot straight up in the air some fifty or sixty feet and hung there for a while before floating back to earth, returning inevitably to the exact spot where it had taken off – either that or the wind took hold of it and carried it along the esplanade. Within an hour, I had made two bus-ride journeys to retrieve the wretched thing.

I did manage to buy a cricket bat, some stumps and a tennis ball though, and we made several abortive attempts to play beach cricket. I think there must have been something wrong with the wicket. When I bowled overarm, the ball left my hand, curved, plopped into the sand and disappeared from view. My four-year-old retrieved it with his wooden spade. When I switched to underarm, the ball left my hand, ploughed a shallow furrow through the sand and slowed to a halt some ten yards from the batsman's reach.

Unfortunately, there weren't enough of us in the family to form a quorum for rounders. Disillusionment, coupled with the weather, forced us to give up beach games entirely.

The third day after our arrival, my seven-year-old discovered an electronic football machine on a pier. You put in 10p and an electronic white blob of a ball pinged back and forth around a screen while you jiggled a little wheel that controlled an electronic white blob that represented a goalkeeper. The machine gave off an electronic humming noise. The seven-year-old became quite proficient at the game; despite his tender years he seems to have a *penchant* for electronic things. When I was his age, even clockwork motors left me cold and baffled. When I was his age, all pier machines cost a penny, and a pre-decimal one at that.

I am twelve years old. I am wearing a school blazer and my first pair of long flannel trousers. I am standing on tip-toe in order to peer through the narrow eyepiece of a cumbersome pier contrivance on metal legs that is labelled Parisienne Nites. *I turn a handle, slowly at first, and inside the box a stocky lady with tight permed curls begins to take off a long chemise, with jerky movements of her hands revealing plump white flesh between corset and silk-stocking-top. . . .*

Boys will be boys.

There are times when I think I will be glad when my two lads reach puberty. I feel that I shall start to understand them then.

INDEX